THE COLTURE PLAYBOOK: VOL 2

A ~~MUSIC~~ BUSINESS GUIDE TO
WEALTH AND INDEPENDENCE

Ty Baisden & Yoh Phillips

Series Creator and Editor, Ty Baisden & Yoh Phillips.

Editor, Venessa Gonzalez.

Book design by Jayne Andrew & Aceani Michelle.

ISBN   979-8-9954031-0-4 (paperback)
ISBN   979-8-9954031-1-1 (ebook)

To the young entrepreneurs.

PLAYBOOK CONTENTS

PROLOGUE

Volume 1 of The **COLTURE** Playbook introduced Ty Baisden—a former athlete who, after a football injury derailed his dreams of playing in the NFL, turned entrepreneur and record executive. Yoh, a music journalist writing for the music blog DJBooth, first interviewed Ty in 2017, when he was a promising record executive, who started a holding company, **COLTURE**, and been working alongside the hottest R&B newcomer in the music industry, Brent Faiyaz, as more than a manager, but a 50-50 business partner.

The interview with Ty was one of Yoh's most viral profiles. Artists, managers, A&Rs, executives, and countless readers reacted to how candidly he spoke about the music business for him and Brent, and how they had built their status without signing a record deal or being directly supported by a major label.

Since 2017, Ty and Yoh have conducted interviews, podcasts, and written a book in hopes of educating future executives, creatives, artists, and entrepreneurs on what it takes to build a company independent of a major record label or to be independent of someone else's money. In **COLTURE** Playbook Volume 1, they dug into some of Ty's backstory and spoke with his close associates about how **COLTURE** began. They also explained the necessary mentality and tools to start your journey as an independent company. **The COLTURE Playbook Volume 2 goes even further into what it takes to maintain and maximize your independence.**

But to understand a major stepping stone for Ty and his company **COLTURE**, we must rewind to December 16, 2016, when GoldLink released the single "Crew" (featuring Brent Faiyaz and Shy Glizzy). What began as a local SoundCloud loosie became a 5x platinum, Grammy-nominated hometown anthem—and Brent's first feature. For Ty, it was the beginning of learning how to leverage, be patience, and say "no" to short-term wins. Below is his unfiltered account of how it happened. This Q&A is based on Ty's recollection, not an exact oral history. Don't be mad at Yoh.

THE "CREW" EFFECT: A RETROSPECTIVE.

Yoh: Did you know "Crew" would blow up?

Ty: Freeze and I were on the phone and I told him, "I don't know what's going to happen with this "Crew" record, but it's either going to go two ways: It's going to turn into a crazy record, and GoldLink is going to have a hard time following up with it, OR, it's just going to be some culture shit that people just fuck with, but I don't care about any of those things…What I care about is how Brent looks."

I tell Freeze, "We're going start doing acoustic performances in so many different places so that people know that Brent's a singer, and we will only perform that record when it's important." You have to realize Yoh, Brent has only performed "Crew" with Goldlink three times—Coachella, Jimmy Fallon, and GoldLink's DC homecoming—that's it.

Y: When "Crew" was made, who facilitated it?

T: I had been chasing Henny [Yegezu] down for Brent and GoldLink to work for a year-and-a-half because they're from the same DMV area. I got fucking emails and text messages chasing Henny down from like, pretty much, late 2014 up until early 2016 when it happened.

Y: So it took almost two years to facilitate.

T: Yeah, and at that time, we had already signed a publishing deal with PULSE. GoldLink had signed to that same pub company. Ashley Calhoun signed both of them, so Ashley was able to add more value to it and, you know, it came together between me, Tunji [Balogun], Henny, and Ashley facilitating, but I literally hounded Henny for a year-and-a-half to get them in the studio together. It was a false start a few times before it actually came together.

Y: Once you had "Crew," did you hear it and know it would be a huge record, or did it start moving, and then you knew it would become a hit?

T: Yeah, and at that time, we had already signed a publishing deal with PULSE. GoldLink had signed to that same pub company. Ashley Calhoun signed both of them, so Ashley was able to add more value to it and, you know, it came together between me, Tunji [Balogun], Henny, and Ashley facilitating, but I literally

hounded Henny for a year-and-a-half to get them in the studio together. It was a false start a few times before it actually came together.

Y: Once you had "Crew," did you hear it and know it would be a huge record, or did it start moving, and then you knew it would become a hit?

T: Nah, Henny and I, were trying to get that record out in the summer of 2016. Henny, at the time, had started managing Shy Glizzy. So that's how Shy Glizzy got on the record. Henny told me he wanted to get the record out during the summer, and it could be a DC thing. He told me he was going to get the radio to support it and it could just be some local, cool culture shit. It wasn't even going to be on the album…Me, I didn't really give a fuck. I'm just trying to get the record out. Me being so green at the time, you have to realize Yoh, I'm green, I'm still learning. So I'm like fuck it, bro, I ain't gonna charge no money. We can just swap. GoldLink can give us a verse later, whatever… Then everything goes dark.

Y: Dark?

T: Yeah, I'd say, around November, the conversation popped back up again. If you follow the timetable of that record, they just dropped the record. Then, not that far along, they dropped the record he had with Jazmine Sullivan ["Meditation."]

They had to push "Crew" because it was performing so crazy at the DSPs [Digital Service Providers]. So they were forced to push it, and that's why it made the GoldLink album [At What Cost]. Initially, if I can remember correctly, Henny was trying to drop it as some cool, SoundCloud culture shit because that's how GoldLink came up, off Soundcloud. So I really wasn't tripping. I was like, shit, nigga, I'm just trying to get the marketing dollars. I was just trying to get the record in the market, I didn't know how big it would be. I didn't think it would be a 4 or 5x times platinum record.

Y: Especially on a feature because Brent doesn't do a lot of features.

T: That was his first feature.

Y: Once the record dropped, what happened next?

T: The record dropped, and that same month, this is before we went to Australia, I talked to Freeze and said, "I'm gonna make it so that he is seen as a singer and not a rapper-singer. So we started doing So Far Sound, which is an acoustic performance. We went to Sundance Film Festival and did an acoustic set and one for ASCAP's showcase.

If you look online, one of Brent's biggest videos from So Far Sound is him performing "Poison." We did So Far Sound in LA, we did So Far Sound in San Francisco. We did probably three or four key acoustic performances to show that he's a singer and not a rapper just doing melody shit. And I purposely did not let him do any performances of "Crew" unless they mattered.

Y: How do you gauge when a performance matters? Especially since he was a new artist. He was very new. actually. Some people would have oversaturated the market in your position.

T: Nigga, Coachella, matters. Late Night Jimmy Fallon matters. The sold-out show GoldLink had in DC, back-to-back sold-out nights, when I wanted to make sure Brent made a presence in his hometown, that matters.

Y: Did you get other offers?

T: Hell yeah! Henny called me at least once or twice a month, like, yo, this offer came in and they want to pay Brent and GoldLink... Yeah, I turned all that shit down.

Y: You turned it all down?

T: Yeah. We made no money off "Crew" going out to a club, off a live show, or a walkthrough. We made no money off that shit."

Y: What are you betting on when you make these choices? When you're saying no to money?

T: I'm betting on brand value and brand capital. When a person sees Nike, they just know it's worth something. It ain't about how many shoes Nike can sell at this point, cause their brand is worth something. So if they don't sell a lot of shoes this year or next year, but in the third year they sell double the amount, it's still Nike. I already knew the niggas voice was unique. So if a fan wants to see this nigga sing, they gotta come to his show, period.

Y: I feel like that was risky, man.

T: All this shit risky man, it's the fucking music business.

GoldLink followed the "Crew" release with a viral music video in March and a remix with Gucci Mane in June. By December 2017, "Crew" was platinum, had peaked at No.45 on the Billboard Hot 100, and every major music website placed the unexpected hit on their year-end lists for "Best Songs of 2017." A

January nomination for Best Rap/Sung Performance at the 60th Grammy Awards further solidified "Crew" as a special record.

Never in the history of rap music had three Black artists, all from the DMV, all underground, end up on a song as massive or wide-reaching as "Crew". And of those three artists, only Brent Faiyaz, who sang the hook, was independent. Not because he had to be, major record labels made their offers, but Ty declined them all. To those who may think a big record means big money, remember, "Crew," is GoldLink's song, not Brent Faiyaz. When the record blew up, Brent and Ty were still working independently without a major record deal.

After the 2018 Grammy Awards, a major Brent tour was scheduled to begin. Ty was entering the next phase of his life, which he discusses extensively in this book. Without further ado, I hand you over to WorldWide Ty.

Like Volume I, he starts this book with *Discipline*.

Chapter 1
DISCIPLINE

— Dr. Dre

The phrase 'lapse of judgment' usually describes a bad decision or mistake caused by a lack of judgment or thought. For example, "His lapse of judgment cost the company millions of dollars in lost revenue."

Now, if a lapse of judgment cost that company millions, what would happen if better choices with fewer mistakes were made? It is safe to say that the company would be in a better position for future growth. See, that is how discipline works. When appropriately applied, discipline positions you and your business in a better position to have future success. Discipline is purely an investment in your future. Yes, you will see results in real time, but overall, the lion's share of the results will improve your future results.

So, is it more valuable to better understand delayed gratification versus the viral approach? Obviously, in 2025, everyone is trying to make it viral. I mean we can just say fuck discipline as a whole and just TikTok, Reel, and X (formally known as Twitter) ourselves to greatness. Who needs hard work when you have social media and a monetized account? Why sharpen your skills when you can just use ChatGPT to take the shortcut? We love a good shortcut. The only issue is that the same technology that helps you with shortcuts will be the same technology that gives you a false sense of education.

The moral of the story is that with the advancement of technology, humans must be more disciplined. When your co-worker who understands how to use tech and computers shows up to take your job, the only thing that will save you is your long-standing practice of discipline, willingness to adapt, and proven results. Artificial intelligence will shake the lazy tree and be the root for the disciplined hard worker.

If I'm honest, this A.I. shit be having me feeling like Iron Man. It truly elevates my skill sets. Still, in the relentless pursuit of excellence, discipline is my compass. Discipline is not the enemy of freedom; instead, it's the very foundation that allows freedom to flourish. It is the structure that strengthens my ambitions, the framework upon which I have built my dreams. Yes, we build our dreams (we will speak on this later).

Discipline is the silent affirmation that echoes in the stillness of my resolve, telling me that I am capable, worthy, and on the right path. In the tapestry of life, each thread of discipline weaves a pattern of success. It's the early mornings spent in the quiet solitude of study and the late nights spent poring over plans and projections. It's the decision to say no to distractions, to focus on the task at hand with laser-like precision while still getting the correct amount of sleep.

DISCIPLINE IS THE ULTIMATE SELF-RESPECT

It's easy to mistake discipline for rigidity and to view it as a barrier to creativity. But in truth, discipline liberates creativity. It provides the boundaries which imagination can roam freely. A disciplined approach to learning and refining my skills allows me to innovate and adapt. Discipline doesn't stifle; it empowers. It transforms potential into prowess and aspiration into achievement.

In this age of instant gratification, discipline is the counterculture. It's the choice to build something enduring rather than ephemeral. It's the understanding that true greatness isn't a product of chance but a result of choice—the choice to do the hard things, make the sacrifices, and walk the path less traveled. And it's this choice that sets the disciplined apart from the crowd.

Discipline is the guardian of my time and the steward of my resources. It's the voice that urges me to invest in myself and cultivate habits that will serve me today and all my tomorrows. It's the recognition that every action I take is a brick in the edifice of my future and that with each disciplined act, I am building a legacy that will stand the test of time.

So let us not shy away from discipline. Let us embrace, celebrate, and recognize it for what it truly is: The most profound expression of self-respect.

For it is through discipline that we declare to the world—and ourselves—that we are committed to living a life of purpose, a life of impact, a life that truly matters, a soft life.

I have learned that to get the soft life, one must go through a disciplined life, which means you must earn your soft life. Funny thing is, I just learned about soft life in 2023. Shit, my life is not soft at all. The shit is hardcore discipline and when you are in the season of discipline you will only have soft life days to balance out the work. You work towards the soft life, and discipline is the fast track to a soft life. I will explain why.

When we pay close attention to human behavior and interactions, we are our own worst enemy on a daily basis. We create self-inflicted wounds based on our daily decisions. Let me give you an example from my own life. Over the years, I have gathered that being out after 11 p.m. drastically increases the chances that some fuck shit will happen when you are a Black men in America.

When I then begin to think of what business deals I can close at a loud ass bar or club at midnight on a Wednesday, is when I discovered the theory of self-inflicted wounds that we created for ourselves. I started to look at discipline differently. When you live without a strategy, applying discipline is extremely difficult. We can't keep fooling ourselves into thinking we can build long-term success without the foundation that discipline develops. In The Colture Playbook Volume 2, discipline is just as important, if not more, as in Volume 1.

Discipline increases daily productivity.
Discipline increases daily confidence.
Discipline increases daily learning curves.

Join me on this journey through 'The Colture Playbook Volume 2', as I guide you from the early days of 2018 to the top of March 2020. Let's explore the business, life's ups and downs, and the clarity that comes from chaos, all through the lens of unwavering discipline.

CAUTIONARY TALE: DON'T BULLSHIT WHILE YOU ON THE CLOCK

A cautionary tale is a story, often in folklore, that warns of danger. It aims to teach a moral lesson and encourage good behavior.

On March 29th, 1988, Will Smith and DJ Jazzy Jeff released their second album, *He's the DJ, I'm the Rapper*. The album went three times platinum and won them the first-ever Grammy Award for Best Rap Performance at the 31st Annual Grammy Awards.

The success made them feel their next album, *And in This Corner...*, should be recorded where other multi-platinum artists made music—specifically, Compass Point Studios, in the Bahamas.

James Lassiter, their manager and voice of reason, was against it. He suggested they record some of the album in Philadelphia, where Jeff built a studio in his mom's basement, and do some sessions in London, where their label, Jive, had a studio and could guarantee the kind of rates to make this the most cost-effective music.

The artists resisted, outvoting management, and flew to the Bahamas with a crew of ten for six weeks of recording. They burned through $10,000 a day, using the studio to entertain women, drink alcohol, and create a nightclub vibe rather than a serious work environment.

When James mentioned their lack of discipline, they said he didn't understand the "creative process." After 30 days and a couple of hundred thousand dollars spent, Will and Jeff had failed to complete a single song. James decided to call Will's dad, who came to the Bahamas, and scolded them all the way back to Philly.

In his book, *Will*, the Fresh Prince wrote how his dad told them: "You boys are fucking off an opportunity that most people can't even dream about. You got a major corporation financin' your project, and you got girls and shit sitting around in the studio? Keep your dick out them people's money. You can bullshit, just don't bullshit while you on the clock. This shit ain't gonna last forever."

They finished *And in This Corner...* two weeks later. Released on October 31, 1989, the album did not live up to it's predecessor and was considered a commercial flop. Their lack of discipline largely to blame. Learn from them. Don't let success disrupt your discipline.

Chapter 2

WORK ETHIC

Wtf is work ethic? Who made this shit up?

In Catholic churches, Protestants consider work ethic a religious importance attached to laboring at one's job. Their definition of work ethic places a high value on productivity and frugality and a negative value on those who do not work hard or try to succeed at their jobs. Puritan ministers discovered this way of life in the 17th century.

So, work ethic is a way of life. If used properly, it is a fundamental cornerstone of changing one's life and one's bloodline.

So, when does work ethic apply? How do I know I'm using it correctly? I, Ty Baisden, don't have the answer, but I have a few personal recommendations to help an individual answer the question.

When a driven work ethic powers your purpose and what you are passionate about, you are using it correctly. Work ethic applies when trying to better yourself as a human and business person. When I lack confidence, I lean heavily on my work ethic. When short on funding, I lean heavily on my work ethic. Having a strong work ethic drives a person to accomplish their goals quickly.

Since we know what work ethic is now, I can tell y'all some shit. In 2018, Brent Faiyaz had a real buzz. Labels wanted to do business with us, and we went on our first world tour. The tour had four legs. The first leg was the A and B markets. We had a two-week break and then went on four European dates. Then we announced the second leg of the tour, B and C markets. Then we did four dates in Australia. All those dates were rough on the body, and the tour was not profitable. We still worked like we were going to make one million dollars.

If you read Colture Playbook Volume 1, you might recall how I had a job working at Delta. I finished working my required 40 hours per week at Delta by the first week of January, then went directly into final preparation for the tour. The Grammys were in New York that year, so we had to prep the tour bus in Los Angeles, California, and then fly to New York City for the Grammys. The entire touring party took the bus to Chicago (if my memory serves me correctly), the first stop. Those who attended the award show flew in after the Grammys and started the tour.

The amount of man-hours we invested in January and February 2018 to properly set up the tour was intense. All this was before our other management team members were there to help us. It was just Freeze, Fabe, and Zoo helping me. I was still a one-person management and label team at that time. I had to attend all rehearsals to ensure the live band was on point. Thaddeus was the music director at the time, and he was excellent at ensuring we had everything, which did help me out a lot.

WHEN HUSTLE OUTWEIGHS LOGIC: THE $15,000 MERCH GAMBLE

Let's talk about what went wrong. I put so many vinyl, cassette tapes, and merch on the bus that there wasn't a lot of room for people to move around. I had spent $15,000 on merchandise alone. All that shit was coming with us. We couldn't afford to ship anything. That was how we planned to make the extra money while on the road, but we ordered too much merchandise and it didn't all fit on the tour bus, so I forced it. So the first four cities were very uncomfortable. There was merch everywhere on the bus. Not to mention we had a support act, so I had to act as a tour manager for Diana Gordon and her band members.

Then, the bus was too big. It was too big because these venues had an average capacity of 250 people. Therefore, none of the venues had parking lots, and no parking was available. This strategy wasn't the most thought-out.

There was no way I could have pulled that off without a very focused work ethic. I didn't go out, nor did I have a bunch of women I was juggling. I was hyper-focused on the tour, and my work ethic was very active during that time frame. I later learned that the work put in during that time would become the foundation for Brent's overall touring business moving forward.

Along with a very aggressive work ethic, I gained support from two PR people named Sandy Abuah (UK) & Lauren Camp (US).

Lauren helped us book the Vice News piece. Sandy helped build the UK PR story for Brent and his band Sonder. With Vice, the camera crew jumped on the tour bus with us for two or three days. I had to manage the tour, load in, set up a merch booth, do sound checks, and be the talent while they interviewed me the whole time. I felt like Tyler Perry in those moments.

There is also something very important to mention: A great work ethic does not equal knowing how to run a successful business. We will get into what that means later in the book. The moral of the story is that at the end of the day, the work never ends.

THE RIPPLE EFFECT: HOW YOUR WORK ETHIC LIFTS EVERYONE AROUND YOU

But let's talk about why work ethic is so vital. It's the engine that drives success, no matter the field. You can have all the talent in the world, but without a strong work ethic, that talent can go to waste. Work ethic means showing up, putting in the hours, and going the extra mile. It's about perseverance in the face of obstacles and focusing on your goals. It's what separates the dreamers from the achievers.

Think about it—every major breakthrough, every significant achievement, is backed by relentless hard work. Sleepless nights, sacrifices, and grinding daily are the hallmarks of a solid work ethic. It's not glamorous and not always fun, but it's necessary. When you commit to a strong work ethic, you commit to progress. You commit to growth.

And it's not just about personal gain. A strong work ethic sets a standard for those around you. It inspires your team, your family, and your community. It creates a culture of excellence that can uplift and transform. So, if you ever wonder why you should bother putting in the extra effort, remember that your work ethic isn't just about you. It's about creating a legacy of diligence, resilience, and success.

CAUTIONARY TALE: WHILE THEY PARTIED, HE WORKED

On August 26, 1993, Tupac Shakur performed at the Metropolis Night Club in Cleveland, Ohio. Before his performance, an announcer introduced the opening act, who he called "Mr. P, the country singer." The opener was not a country singer, but New Orleans rapper Master P.

As one of P's first-ever concerts as a performer, what he remembers most about that night is how everyone was there to see Tupac and were unmoved by his songs, except for one guy in the crowd who bounced to his entire set. When P saw him, he said to himself, "I'm going to turn that one fan into millions."

So, how does a southern rapper with no industry notoriety open up for Tupac? It starts with Master P seeing a future in music from every possible angle: Artist, producer, and entrepreneur.

P's breakthrough into the music business began with a move from New Orleans to Richmond, California, where he opened a retail record store called No Limit Records using the money from a malpractice suit following the death of Sergeant Claude Miller, his grandfather. This grandfather, a veteran who fought in the Vietnam War, inspired the No Limit name after telling Master P to start his own business, to start his own army.

Bay Area rappers Too Short, E-40, Spice-1, and Tupac would come through Master P's record store and tell him he could be a rapper, too. Performing on the road helped boost this belief, but Master P knew he wasn't the best rapper and if he was to become a better rapper, the studio had to become his second home.

What set P apart wasn't pure talent, but how he wasn't afraid to outwork everybody. While Tupac and all the guys were out partying, playing, and having fun, he was in the studio. While they slept, he worked. Doing so without a major record deal or any backing besides his own. His grandfather instilled this independent drive and aggressive hustle early in life, telling him, "You're not going to make it in their system; you have to create your own."

By 1998, at the age of 28, Master P and No Limit Records were among the biggest independent record labels in the world.

Chapter 3
DON'T DRINK THE KOOL-AID

Being successful in the music industry can be confusing as fuck. You could win a GRAMMY while having an incredible work ethic, but have four roommates, a bad record deal, and no funds in your bank account. Please don't get me wrong, there's absolutely nothing wrong with having four roommates because that can be a great way to save money while you are grinding, but usually that isn't the case.

The point I'm making is that you can win a prestigious award, and this award implies that you are successful within the music business, while your business dealings aren't in your favor, and your income doesn't match your perceived success. What does all of this really mean? Why can you appear successful but not make money that helps you feel successful and secure on the inside? Welcome to the music business, nigga, the land of cappin'. Cap me down town!

When you remove the brunches, pictures with celebrities, egos, designer clothes, Uber SUVs, Airbnb mansions, fake jewelry, fake followers, fake streams, and no hard skills or soft skills, it only leaves you with a tall glass of Kool-Aid.

Do you know the history behind 'Don't drink the Kool-Aid?' Ok, a quick history lesson.

The Jonestown Massacre of 1978 remains a chilling illustration of the devastating consequences of cult manipulation and isolation. Over 900 people perished under the influence of Jim Jones, the leader of the Peoples Temple cult, who convinced his followers to relocate to Jonestown, Guyana, and ultimately orchestrate a mass murder-suicide. Jones's charismatic but manipulative personality fueled an environment of complete control, isolating his devotees from the outside world.

This tragic event serves as a fuckin reminder of the exploitation that can occur within our communities if we invite the wrong energy. Parallels can be drawn between the manipulative tactics of cult leaders and those employed by certain individuals in the music industry. Young and aspiring artists, eager for success, can be particularly susceptible to being taken advantage of by managers, producers, or record labels.

Shit, some of these niggas can be taken advantage of themselves because they are so blind to their own shortcomings as well. These figures may exert undue control over an artist's career, finances, and even personal life, mimicking the control Jim Jones wielded over his followers in Jonestown.

Artists must be aware of the potential for exploitation within the industry to safeguard themselves. Surrounding themselves with trustworthy advisors and learning how to be their own legal counsel (while working with a lawyer as well) can be powerful defenses against manipulative tactics. Building a strong community and maintaining a healthy dose of skepticism is essential for navigating the often complex world of music.

One of my business partners said to me one day, "Ty, if they don't trust these people, why do they act like they can't fire them?" Man, I didn't even have a real answer for the nigga. I said some shit like "Man maybe they feel like they will fuck up their career or some shit."

This brings me to another point. Please fire anyone who feels like they do not have your best interest as an artist or business owner. If you are always high and distracted, you will never notice who is for you or against you. Become a student of this game and of business overall, because you could easily be the sweet lick for the Kool-Aid.

The money is hard to make and harder to keep, so everyone has to be there to serve the community equally. We are case studies of when a boutique community creates multiple millionaires off of art. It is possible and easy to maintain when everyone understands the mission.

MOMENTUM > HYPE: WHY WE NEVER DRANK THE KOOL-AID

Los Angeles changed my life, and I'm forever grateful for that city, but L.A. is what I call the Kool-Aid Capital. There is so much red Kool-Aid to drink in L.A. If you don't have an identity before you get to L.A., you will have one projected on you, especially if you achieve success quickly.

I was lucky that I didn't have time to get caught up at the Kool-Aid drinking parties. There was too much work to do. Brent was too busy in the studio every day, still adjusting to all the moving parts of being a hot up-and-coming artist.

We never lost sight of who we wanted to be while working to kick-start our business. Since we didn't spend much time in Kool-Aid Land, our support team didn't, either. We were all just excited that something we worked on that nobody cared about was growing. We focused on the momentum we were building and didn't let the industry stuff get to us. It started with me as the manager.

During these times, I realized how important being a manager is, especially when you build the business independently. I was in charge of providing everything with proper structure and ensuring everyone got paid fairly.

One of the biggest factors that helped our community was how Brent didn't receive better treatment than anyone else. We found that perfect balance where everyone was valued equally for a long time. We operated as a team, sharing resources and celebrating our success together. Everyone's life benefited positively from this approach. We worked every day while looking out for each other. Daily.

One of the best moments has always been watching everyone get paid on the 15th of every month from Stem. We would call these checks 'That Stemmy.' Anytime a new project or producer was introduced to the team, we knew they would get hit with 'That Stemmy.' Each project would spike that Stemmy check.

"Stem Is the label that pays me," would be some shit I would say out loud. We was off the Work-Aid, not the Kool-Aid.

CAUTIONARY TALE: THE ILLUSION OF IMPORTANCE—AND WHAT ACTUALLY MATTERS

"I drank the Kool-Aid several times," actor Steve Guttenberg admitted when the website Page Six asked if he ever fell victim to the charm and temptations of Hollywood. "I had my times when I thought I was a big deal, I went out and bought a Ferrari," he confessed before sharing what the Kool-Aid drunk taught him about life.

"You get to the end of that tunnel and realize you're not that big a deal and nobody's that big a deal, right? The biggest star in the world, is not a big deal. The biggest CEO in the world is not a big deal, right? Because we're fungible. We're human, right? We have a limited amount of time to dance on this earth. Try to do the right thing all the time. Try to be nice to people. Be kind. Be thoughtful. Everything else works out."

Chapter 4
PLAY STUPID GAMES & WIN STUPID PRIZES

Aiming to run a successful business without seeking education is an example of playing stupid games. The byproduct of that is entering a bad business deal, which, my good people, is what we call winning a stupid prize.

In this chapter, we are at the beginning of 2019, the company is coming off a successful tour run in Australia, and labels are still hitting us up offering deals. I decided to re-evaluate all of our business dealings at the time. I first looked at how we could hire a digital person, increase the team's pay, and save funds for investing back into the business.

STRATEGY OVER LUCK: THE CALCULATED MOVES THAT GREW OUR BUSINESS

I had three strategies that I was going to roll out to increase the company's revenue for 2019 and 2020. The first was to look at our distribution business closely. The entire year of 2018, we had a handshake deal with Human Re Sources, a music distribution and services company with label services, on an 80/20 deal.

The partnership was amazing, and Human Re Sources founder J. Erving kept his word on every single thing he said he would do for us. I was extremely grateful for the experience and community. So many times, I had to call them for advice, and they always answered my calls, but I knew I needed that 20% back to scale our business for the next 24 months.

We never removed any of the music we did with Human Re Sources, but with the new releases, we went back to the Sonder Son days, Brent's debut album, which we distributed through Lost Kids using only Stem. That decision was the beginning of the business's growth because now I had more revenue to hire internal staff to work around the clock.

The second strategy to increase company revenue was officially launching our online merchandise business. It wasn't until the third quarter of 2019 that we officially launched the Lost Kids online merchandise store. Before then, we were only selling merch when we toured. This approach did create a demand for the merchandise over the years. We left money on the table for years, but it created hype around the products, which was the trade-off. We created hype in many ways, but it was unintentional. Our lack of knowledge or slow learning sometimes made us look like geniuses, but we were just learning different parts of the business.

The company's third revenue growth strategy was to figure out the world of YouTube monetization. It took me a very long time to figure this out. I always wondered how these Vloggers made so much money on YouTube. At this time, investing more money into the music videos was a thing that Brent was very passionate about, so the YouTube piece was very important for me to figure out.

I wasn't sold on investing a bunch of money into music videos. Still, I figured that revenue would fund the music videos if we could monetize his YouTube channels properly. Needless to say, I didn't figure this out quickly, you will learn about this in Colture Playbook Vol 3.

BROKE AT 50 IS A CHOICE: STOP PLAYING WITH YOUR REVENUE

Making a good amount of revenue and spending it on dumb items is another example of playing stupid games and winning stupid prizes. The stupid prize in this example would be not having the funds to grow your business, and then getting a loan from a major label. We positioned ourselves so that it was always easy to say "no" to opportunities that didn't make sense for the business.

I remember Brent and I bought two Rolexes as Christmas gifts. One for his dad, and I bought one for my brother. We didn't have watches for ourselves at the time, nor did we have a car. Brent bought his parents a house before he had a car or a watch. During those moments, we were just trying to put the money where it felt it should be. We were investing the bulk of the money into payroll and creatives, aka intellectual property. We were in the catalog business, so everything was about building the catalog.

We didn't want to play any stupid games with how we handled our intellectual property. I knew it was so important to always keep control over our catalog so that we could leverage it when we needed to. I will be the first to tell you that making money on a monthly basis off your business is tough, and making money off music every month is even more difficult. I couldn't allow myself to blow the money in a wasteful way.

I need to say to all young artists and business owners, please be great stewards of your revenue. It is hard to make money off your art, so honor it when you do. Don't blow it. The money doesn't come at the same pace forever. You have to understand how to invest and maintain it. Getting money in your 20s and 30s but being broke in your 50s and 60s is definitely a stupid prize.

PLAY STUPID GAMES WITH YOUR ARTIST? ENJOY YOUR STUPID PRIZE

If you're spending the same amount of money your artist is spending but only making 20% of what they make, you're playing stupid games, and you'll get a stupid prize.

If you want to keep your client but you're having sex with the same women as your client, you smoke dope with them, and you drink with them, you're playing stupid games and you're going to get a stupid prize.

You have to be conscious of what you work for and what you don't work for. You can get a prize for not working. You can get a prize for coming in 12th place. You don't want to come in 12th place if you're trying to be the primary manager for a client.

I say this because people get it misconstrued in business relationships. I'll use Brent as an example. Brent listened to me because, at that time, I was resourceful enough for him to trust that I was less likely to be wrong. I never took advantage of that. Me taking advantage of that is playing stupid games.

At this point, Brent doesn't need me. He decided to continue doing business with me. I take that my good faith in trying to be very, very forthcoming about percentages, how I viewed the business, and how I took less to make sure he and the company had more, reflected in how he moved around me.

Understand the talent needs you until they don't. Never forget that, so you can always remember: Even when they need you, you should treat them like they don't need you. Because the moment that you miss that mark, the moment you think that you are the sole reason they're where they're at, based on how you act and talk to them, it's going to impact your business in a way that's so detrimental. Because in the early stages, the stakes are not as high.

The stakes get really high when you're successful together, then everyone wants to come in and give you deals and have all these different conversations.

So you have to have foresight, something I don't think a lot of managers have. I don't think a lot of artists have it either. Some artists I worked with in the past didn't have foresight and didn't treat me as well as they should have. Now their careers don't look like my career. That's not a shot at them. That's a real thing. You have to understand the people who surround you. You might be working with the next star and they're just getting out of college. They're interning for the moment. They may be interning for your manager.

So don't get big-headed, that's a self-fulfilling prophecy. I know people who caught a wave, and nobody liked them anymore because of how they treated people, just because they had something hot. And when that shit wasn't hot no more, people remembered it. They remembered how you treated them.

CAUTIONARY TALE: THE FINANCIAL DISCIPLINE BEHIND OUR SOUND

"Ty and I were discussing how Lost Kids was the first time Ty, as a manager, had the majority control over an artist's business. Ty never thought he had majority control over the music, even though Brent granted him power in the creative process. Ty was never forceful about the creative. If Brent wanted to do something artistic, outside of spending huge budgets on music videos, Ty was supportive.

Although confident that he never impeded on what Brent wanted to do creatively, for historical accuracy, he called Brent to fact-check his remembrance of things." – Yoh.

Ty: I got a question for you.

Brent: What's going on?

T: I'm writing Colture Playbook Vol. 2. Outside of being stingy with the music video budgets, was there anything else I did to impede your creativity?

B: Sampling!

T: Sampling, that's what it was! Because sampling would be expensive, and we

were broke. And Brent would be like, 'But everybody samples,' and I would be like, 'But everybody broke!'

The album that just came out [*Larger Than Life*], I had nothing to do with the creative process at all. Brent completely controlled it, and it had the most samples. I think he didn't give a fuck about making money off the art, but more so about being able to sample…

Yoh: As an expression.

T: Yes. You see how fast he said that shit, samples!

Y: He remembered.

T: When we were in the Dominican Republic doing the first album [Sonder Son], I was in that bitch walking around like a drill sergeant. Don't be sampling shit in here! Don't be sampling shit! We can't afford that shit!

Y: Brent, did you feel like you couldn't make the music you wanted because Ty said no sampling? Or did you have to find another way of making it?

B: I just had to find another way to do it. One thing about sampling: you have a reference already there, so it allows you to make music at a quicker rate. Making music from scratch takes way more time.

T: Way more time.

B: But we didn't really have a problem finding a sound or making shit the way we wanted to.

T: You know what's so crazy; I didn't know it was going to happen like this, but because we didn't sample at all, until, shit, maybe Wasteland and a few samples on Fuck The World, but because of that, everybody calls to sample Brent. I wasn't thinking about it at that time, I was just thinking, we ain't had no motherfucking money, and sampling was going to make us go broke.

Y: Now you're in the position to clear samples?

T: We get sample requests all the time.

B: We ended up being the sample.

Chapter 5
SHINY PRISON

I ran into my patna and his homie a while ago when they were out kickin' it. His homie just got a new job. It was something he was real excited about.

After working there for some years, he wasn't so happy anymore. Not being happy didn't stop him from getting raises. I don't know his finances, but I'm pretty sure his lifestyle changed with every raise. That is our curse as Black people. We get a raise, we go and buy some new shit.

We don't think about what may change at the company or how the thing we love most about the job could dissolve over time, and now we can't just up and leave because of lifestyle.

When people end up in dynamics like that, where they're in these shiny ass jobs but are unhappy because they haven't set themselves up to be in a better position, I call it a shiny prison.

It's like being in the feds if you are a big-time drug dealer. Federal prisons look way different than your standard prison. When you have access to a certain amount of funds, your prison experience is different, but you are still in prison. A shiny prison, when you have your physical freedom, is a mental thing.

WHEN LIFESTYLE INFLATION LOCKS YOU IN

Let's say you're at a job. You do well at that job. You're $60,000 a year at that job. Your boss loves you and believes you will continue to excel in the company. Next thing you know, you get a raise. You get a $20,000 bump. You get a new title. Now you make $80,000. You're getting close to that twenty-five percentile.

You don't take that $20,000 bump and put it toward stock investments. No, you get a new car. You get a new boo. You get a new apartment. Cause you're up. Again, as Black people, we get a raise, we get new shit.

Fast forward six months. You're living the life, baby. You got the new whip, the new crib, and the new boo. You're probably Uber-eating more than you should. Maybe you go out to the lounges more than you should. And on top of all that, the boss who gave you the raise, the one who loves you, leaves the company. They went and got a new job.

Now you have a new boss. You can't stand this muuuafucka, and that muuuafucka can't stand you. Now you remember how this ain't even your dream job. But you can't leave. How will you pay for the overhead you created? You want to keep the car, right? And keep the crib, right? Shit, your girl needs the new Chanel, don't she? Now you are in a shiny prison. The shiny prison is made from a mismanagement of your actual growth.

DOWNSIZING AS FREEDOM: BREAKING OUT OF YOUR SHINY PRISON

What should you do if you find yourself in a shiny prison? Downsize. It's the key to unlocking that shiny prison cell.

But downsizing means you tell the new boo we are moving from this three-bedroom condo overlooking the L.A. skyline to a one-bedroom in Inglewood. You downsize from the Scat and get the Honda. It will save you some money on the insurance and the car note. You also can't Uber Eats like that anymore. You might realize your new boo can't really cook. Shit, you can't cook either. So now you have to learn.

The food may taste bad. Your car won't be fancy. The relationship might get rocky. I won't say you'll be walking, but you might want to get a bike. It'll keep you fit once the gym membership is gone. But if you stay disciplined and downsize properly, you will slowly open that shiny prison door. It won't feel like it because downsizing can feel like you're out of the feds but in the county jail.

Realistically, once you taste that up, you don't want not to taste that up anymore. Especially when you are choosing to reduce spending, it's one thing to lose it all and be forced to scale down, but to say, I got it, and I'm going to forcefully, intentionally, downsize. That takes discipline. It's not forever, though. It's only to position yourself better.

All this is to highlight that, to get out of the shiny prison, your conditions have to worsen, but your money doesn't get worse. Your money is going to be up. It's only your quality of life, for the moment, that's in the mud. Listen, manure is used to grow plants nigga. If we take the approach that mother nature gives us, it takes some shit to grow.

HOW PERSONAL BAGGAGE BECOMES CAREER LIABILITY

I was once sitting down with Lucian Grainge [CEO of Universal Music Group]. Tunji [CEO of Def Jam Recordings] had set a meeting for me to come in and speak with Lucian about what a partnership could look like. I first said to him, 'I can't stand the music business. It's a lot of terrible people in the music business.' He leaned in and was like, "I agree." I thought that shit was wild. You are the CEO of one of the biggest labels, and you agree with me that these people are terrible.

Lucian told me how artists would come to him when they fired their old manager and were looking for a new one. He never told them who to work with. He will introduce them to people and tell them to ask about their finances. Because if you get a manager with bad finances, they will make bad decisions with yours too. That shit he said gave me clarity on a lot of things. Secondly, Lucian said to ask them if they're divorced, married, or single. Because if they're divorced, they probably got alimony, child support, and a lot of financial things that might not give them the best clarity on making decisions on behalf of your career.

He basically told the artist not to partner with a muuuafucka in shiny prisons. Because if you don't ask these questions, you'll come in thinking the things you're doing will be properly managed when they don't even manage their life properly. If they can't manage their life properly, why in the hell will they be able to manage your career properly?

You must keep your artists out of a shiny prison as a manager. One of the things Brent always tells me is: You cheap man, you cheap. You don't even want to spend any money. Like I said before, Brent likes to spend money on creativity. He'll spend $400,000 on a music video if you let him. Boy, you are crazy. I ain't going in that shiny prison, boy. We are not doing that. I got $50,000. You better figure it out with the 50-piece unless you have some sponsorships.

He doesn't like that I'm cheap about those types of things, but I'm so aware of how we can put ourselves in so much debt that we must do things that we don't want to do. One of the OGs recently told Brent that he's not cheap; he's smart. Being smart will keep you out of the shiny prison.

FUCK YOU MONEY: THE POWER OF WALKING AWAY ON YOUR OWN TERMS

I remember conversing with my business partner, Jayne. Jayne and I were in the apartment hallway arguing. Jayne is really artist-friendly, and I am integral; it just so happens that my integrity often leans artist-friendly sometimes.

So me and her were going back and forth, and I told her, "Every one of these niggas can fire me. I'm gonna go stay with my momma, get my job back at Delta, and in 24 months, I'm back up. Give a fuck about these niggas if they don't give a fuck about me. I'm not changing who I am as a person to represent anybody."

My mom was literally in the living room as I was saying this.

When you get down to the nitty-gritty of it, you can control how you go about your actual journey here on Earth. You can control your emotions, and you can control your actions.

If you have $10 and decide not to spend that by staying home, you control that. Nobody forced you to go out and get a drink. Or go out and buy a new pair of shoes. That's how we should think when we get financial bumps. You are on a quicker path to financial wellness, and financial literacy, aka Fuck You Money, aka the ability to remove yourself when something no longer serves you the sooner you realize that.

CAUTIONARY TALE: FETTY WAP'S SHINY PRISON

On February 27, 2015, Fetty Wap's "Trap Queen" debuted on Billboard's Hot 100 Chart at No. 87. By the 16th of May, "Trap Queen" had reached No. 2, where it peaked, but the single did go No. 1 on Billboard's Hot Rap Song. His breakout single had been out for 11 months, first appearing on SoundCloud, before taking over radio stations nationwide.

"Trap Queen" was certified a Diamond record by the RIAA with over 10 million units sold in the United States on November 8, 2019. Fetty's follow-up single, "679," is 6x-platinum. The Monty-featured, Drake-remixed "My Way" and the single "Again" are both 3x-platinum. These credits show how Fetty Wap was the hottest newcomer in rap and R&B to come out of Patterson, New Jersey.

But success came with a complete lifestyle upgrade: He spent $80,000 fixing his teeth and $2.5 million on jewelry. He also had multiple apartments—four in New Jersey, two in Miami, and a couple in Los Angeles. In addition to what he did for himself, Fetty spent money on others. He bought clothes, took care of flights, and bought 72 cars, 40 of which were for friends and family. At one point, his monthly bills reached $200,000.

Before being sentenced for drug charges in May of 2023, in his final interview, Fetty admitted that he spent over 22 million dollars living in a shiny prison. He didn't realize it until the money was gone, his friends had vanished, and the choices he made attempting to make the money back resulted in a very real incarceration.

Chapter 6

IF YOU NOT AT THE TABLE, YOU ON THE MENU

Think about this: As a businessperson, you have always prided yourself on your entrepreneurial spirit and relentless drive to succeed. You have worked tirelessly for years to grow your business, pouring your heart and soul into every endeavor.

However, despite your best efforts, you couldn't shake off the overwhelming feeling that something was missing; there was a key piece of knowledge or information you simply weren't privy to. It was as if there was an exclusive table where all the power players gathered, making decisions that shaped the industry, and you were left waiting in the shadows, desperate for a seat.

Little did you know that this realization would catalyze a transformative journey to uncover the true meaning behind the saying, "If you're not at the table, you're on the menu."

So here's the thing ... A seat at the table is real, and we would be cappin' you down if we didn't discuss this in Vol 2. Let me be very clear, you can have an amazing career as an artist and manager in the music business without ever having a seat at the "Table." I have done it for years, and I'm happy with my success.

MIDDLEMEN MAKE YOU THE MEAL: WHY INFORMATION CONTROL = POWER

The concept of seat at the table is about information and resources. Not every table is worth sitting at. Some tables are key to knowing about, so you can decide if you want to sit there. There are tables that you and your community create. These are my favorite types of tables. I highly encourage this approach or a mix between your table and a few others.

If you can position yourself not to be the middleman, you're less likely to be on the menu. One of the things I tell my booking agent, one of the things I tell anybody that I'm in business with, I say, hey man, I don't like being the last one to know my business. Because it makes me feel insecure about the source that I'm connected to.

If something is financially happening with my business, I should know it first. But suppose you're in a situation where everything comes through a middleman, who has a middleman, who has another middleman. In that case, it gets to you; you don't have direct access to information, so you aren't treated a certain way.

See, I can call Brent and be like, say bruh, I just got the report back on an evaluation of our catalog. I can tell him, confidently, that the shit is off. I know it's off because I get my money directly from the source. When I say the money I'm getting is directly from the source, I have access to the whole business. I know we have a bunch of loans out. Pretty much all our loans are good loans, but they still need to be worked out so they can be better loans, the greatest loans, but I know how much our company makes every month.

We don't see that amount in real time because we're constantly paying off some of this good debt. I call it good debt because it doesn't collateralize against anything. It doesn't show up on my credit report, and if we default on it, it won't take any of our master ownership away.

Back to my main point: I can tell Brent when the information is inaccurate since I have all this access. Our level of access and control protects us. Controlling our catalog is not being on the menu. You'll never be on the menu when you control your catalog.

BUILD A SYSTEM, STAY OFF THE MENU

I've been talking about this a lot, and in all these different conversations, I try to convince every Black man I speak to not to partner with somebody who might have them on the menu.

I tell them, "Hey man, figure out how to be your own thing, control it, and see about inviting people in." Over the last five weeks, I have told four people this: 'Don't change your system. If you believe in your system, get somebody to invest in it. Tell them, 'I'll take this amount of money, but my system has to stay the same.'

I repeat, keep your system. You never know how impactful your system can be. If you have a system that works for you, you probably just need more money. Find out how to convince those with the money to put money in your system. Build a system, and you'll forever stay off the menu. But if you don't have a system in place, you're basically at the mercy of who has the money. Because that's what money does: money has the ability to change your system. Nothing can be wrong with your system for the record, but you needing money makes it feel like there is something wrong with your system. But a lot of people don't know they can say, hey man, I got a system that works, and if you want to invest in my system, let's do it. They'll be a lot further as artists.

I knew that my system was working when communities started being built: because nothing counts until the money is made.

Let's say I have an artist and I'm doing the right things: Making sure all the producers on the projects have their splits in, and every month they get paid out. Now let's say they're only getting paid a couple hundred dollars monthly. They might not give a fuck about that shit. But, foundationally, all the contracts are in, everybody is getting paid what they agreed upon, they can log into their account, and everything is there, easy breezy.

Let's say I do that same thing, but now the producers are getting between $15,000 to $30,000 monthly. Now it's real. Because when money is made, everything becomes real. It's fucked up because, realistically, it's real even when the money isn't being made.

One of my pet peeves is people calling me about money they're owed. That shit burns me. Especially if we are in business already, I can't stand that shit. I try to make sure motherfuckers are paid, fast. I can't stand motherfuckers calling me about money. If somebody calls me and says they haven't been paid, I think my system isn't working. Now I'm irritated and have to find out why. It's like fixing a bug. Sometimes I know why, other times, shit, something needs to get placed better. Your system gives you clarity.

IF YOUR ARTIST IS ON THE MENU, SO ARE YOU

I can't really speak for myself, because Brent has more power in this particular conversation, but he has the ability as the talent to say, you know what, music is going well, this year I'm not going on the road, instead, he decides to wake up, play GTA for 295 days out of the year, and travel the other 60.

Then, the following year, he can decide to headline a tour, do festivals, host gigs, sell merchandise, and do brand deals. Do all these different things, make all the money he spent that previous year, and profit a 15x multiple.

I don't have that ability, because I'm not the talent. My only ability is to take my money and try to invest in the right things. That's the big difference between Brent and me. If he was on the menu, then I was going to be on the menu until I separated myself from him. So in the early stages of talent management, you can't allow your talent to be on the menu because you're on the menu.

Chapter 7

COLTURE

Let me tell you something—I'm Black, unapologetically so, and when the name COLTURE hit me, I was in Hawaii, showering, thinking of three things: first, God, thank you for this concept. Second, Colt 45 (I know, I don't even drink). Yeah, COLTURE got its name from Colt 45, but I had to flip the spelling to lock down that trademark. And the third thing that came to mind was The Migos because they had this whole "Culture" campaign, and they were out here spelling it all kinds of ways.

I became so invested in the name that I couldn't shake it. I had Wealthy incorporate it in Georgia under COLTURE.Inc., and she helped me build a deck because I was on a mission to raise money for this idea.

Once some companies showed interest, I knew I needed a partner, someone to co-found COLTURE with me. A dude named Dru, who worked at CAA, introduced me to Jayne Andrew. So, with my thick Southern accent, I'm out here trying to explain this vision, and she can't understand half the words coming out of my mouth—but she got the vision. She understood the mission of empowering artists.

Here's the plot twist—COLTURE really came to life when I said, "Nah, I'm good" to all that private investment money. I wanted to build this thing "my way", no strings attached. Lost Kids was me and Brent's company, but Lost Kids was Brent's idea. I was the one putting in the infrastructure and running the marketing machine. But COLTURE? That was "my" vision, something I could ride with for the rest of my time here on Earth. By June 2018, we went deep into the trenches and started to build Lost Kids with COLTURE as the backbone. That's when I had to face the music—I couldn't clock in at Delta anymore. I had a company to build that was about to be positively disruptive to the industry. I was extremely excited and determined.

At that point, COLTURE was just a name with no real meaning. Jayne was on me, like clockwork, asking, "What's the meaning? What story are we telling?" And I'm sitting there like, "Figuring it Out!" All I ever cared about was not getting fired and treating artists right. I'm like, "What story we telling?" Shit, I forreal didn't know why the fuck she was asking me that. We not telling a broke nigga story I know that much. Then one day, on a Delta flight, I was writing ideas down, and then God spoke.

Can
Our
Leverage
Teach
Us
Real
Equity

I looked at Jayne and said, "I got it. I finally got it". Seven words that would define COLTURE, and it took me seven months to land on it. The most important question I ever asked myself became the acronym guiding everything we were building. Man, they're gonna make a movie about this one day. I just hope I'm alive to see it—and please, God, don't let it be corny.

But real talk—being Black, we've never really had the chance to capture true wealth or own the equity in our ideas. Either we got hustled, we gave up too soon, got in conflict with each other in the business, or we sold too quickly. Not this time. Not with COLTURE. We're creating a platform where Black and Brown people can come, thrive, and be whoever they want to be. We're not selling that. We're reinvesting, period.

HOW COLTURE REWRITES THE RULES OF CREATOR EQUITY

From day one, we've had a motto that most folks don't know about: When art is monetized, creators eat first. That means at least 50% of all revenue goes straight to the creators. If a song makes a million dollars, half a million goes to the people who made it. The rest? That's for promotion, services, and management fees. We make sure that every creator who contributes to the catalog is taken care of as long as that music keeps earning. This company is a gift from God, and I will honor that by making the right choices for the people we serve.

As we kept building, I realized COLTURE wasn't just a business but a community movement. A movement that was rewriting the story for Black and Brown creators, especially for our women. It wasn't just about making opportunities. It was about making a lasting impact. There were days when it felt like the struggles would swallow us whole, but the vision kept us pushing forward. We weren't just building a company; we were building a legacy. A family business turned into a corporation, giving back to our community.

COLTURE is about creating that corporate infrastructure with community care at its core. COLTURE ain't just a brand, it's a blueprint for how we shift the lives of millions. We aim to level the playing field across entertainment, media, sports, and technology. It will not be the easiest thing to achieve, but we will continue to keep on building. It is important to me that I do my part while here on earth. COLTURE was born while I focused on music solutions, but as we grow in business, we will focus on multiple solutions across the world. The question that we ask is a global question. **Can Our Leverage Teach Us Real Equity?** Let's not miss the opportunity to answer this question accurately.

Chapter 8
BEING BOUTIQUE

"Boutique" at its core is defined by its commitment to quality over quantity. What else? The willingness to build its own infrastructure in-house. Boutique firms are characterized by their smaller size, which allows them to focus on delivering highly personalized services and niche products. Whether it's a boutique record label, a specialized talent agency, or a custom event production company, the emphasis is always on providing a tailored experience that meets their clients' and audiences' specific needs and desires.

I changed the wording from "indie" to "boutique." First, the wording is sexier and feels expensive. The concept that being indie in music means you must do everything on a shoestring budget isn't true. We wanted to change that way of thinking through our work. Being Boutique has power, and the future is Boutique. Our strategy as a Boutique business was to focus on building one brand for six years and then diversify to strengthen the company's foundation.

Mom-and-pop stores never felt like nice boutique stores. It's the same difference between a thrift store and a premium streetwear store. Both businesses are in the same category as small businesses with fewer than 25 employees. Why does one feel so different than the other? It's not about the product more than it is about the taste and approach to the business. I know for a fact that you can make a thrift store fly and expensive-looking, but that takes intentionality and curation.

In an industry often dominated by sprawling corporations and mass-produced content, boutique businesses in music and entertainment offer a refreshing alternative. These smaller, specialized firms provide a unique blend of personalized service, creative freedom, and niche expertise that starkly contrasts the one-size-fits-all approach of larger entities. Boutique is the future. All business owners and clients want personalized services and are willing to pay more for that level of service.

Our boutique business hit a turning point in February 2020. It felt like all the stars aligned, and the growth was explosive. The truth is, I can't fully explain *how* it all happened—but I've always been clear on the why. And when you know your "why," that's the part you lock in on.

In this case, dissecting the "how" would be a waste of energy. The momentum wasn't about overthinking; it was about doubling down on the purpose, the mission, and the bigger vision. That's where the real value lives—knowing the why so clearly that everything else falls into place. I see so many artists who don't truly understand the value of consistency—delivering a product that looks, smells, and tastes the same every time. You know what I mean? Keeping the winning formula intact. When the fans show you what they love, that's your signal to double down. Don't complicate it. That's your lane. Stay in it.

At the end of the day, we're here to serve the fanbase. That's the *only* way we make a living from this art. But here's where some artists mess up: arrogance. It's easy to start performing for yourself instead of those who show up for you. That's not art; that's masturbation. If you're not teachable as an artist, you'll only focus on what you want, expecting the fans to keep pouring into you with nothing real in return. That's not how this works. It's a two-way street. You have to give just as much as you take.

If someone asked me to spell "When the Stars Align," I'd spell it T-I-K T-O-K—TikTok. Because in today's music business, that's precisely what it means when everything clicks for an artist. One moment, one trend, one viral sound, and their entire world explodes. It's not just about going viral; it's about reaching a new level of success that shifts the whole trajectory of their career. TikTok has become the modern-day definition of alignment in this industry. The fans decide, the culture amplifies, and the doors swing wide open. We knew the play: double down on the sound and stay in the box. Once the fans showed us what they wanted, we didn't overthink it—we leaned in. It was pre-COVID when we were first introduced to the marketing beast we now know as TikTok.

The lesson was simple: Don't fight the audience; serve them. We didn't pivot genres or try to reinvent the wheel. We kept the formula tight and gave the fans exactly what they desired. That was the moment everything shifted. The boutique business we built started scaling globally. It wasn't magic—it was alignment with the fans, the culture, and the platform that connected them to the sound.

THE ESSENCE OF A BOUTIQUE BUSINESS

At its core, a boutique business in music and entertainment is defined by its commitment to quality over quantity. These firms are characterized by their smaller size, which allows them to focus on delivering highly personalized services‧ and niche products. Whether it's a boutique record label, a specialized talent agency, or a custom event production company, the emphasis is always on providing a tailored experience that meets their clients' and audiences' specific needs and desires. This is what we embodied.

PERSONALIZED SERVICE: A HALLMARK OF BOUTIQUE FIRMS

One of the most significant advantages of a boutique business is its ability to offer personalized service. In a boutique setting, clients are not just another number; they are valued partners whose needs and preferences are carefully considered and catered to. This level of personalization can make all the difference in the world of music and entertainment, where individual tastes and unique artistic visions play a critical role.

Consider an emerging musician seeking representation. A boutique talent agency can provide hands-on, individualized career development, working closely with the artist to craft a path that aligns with their goals and aspirations. This bespoke approach is often lost in larger corporations, where standardized processes and sheer volume can dilute the attention given to each client.

AGILITY AND FLEXIBILITY: THE POWER TO PIVOT

The ability to adapt quickly to new trends and changing circumstances is invaluable in the fast-paced and ever-evolving world of music and entertainment. Unburdened by the bureaucratic red tape that often stifles larger organizations, boutique businesses are exceptionally agile. They can pivot their strategies and operations with ease, allowing them to stay ahead of the curve and respond swiftly to the needs of their clients and the market.

This flexibility extends to creative projects as well. Boutique firms can experiment and innovate, taking risks that larger companies might avoid. Boutique firms can lead to groundbreaking work that pushes the boundaries of the industry and sets new standards for creativity and originality.

BUILDING CLOSE RELATIONSHIPS: THE BOUTIQUE ADVANTAGE

The smaller scale of boutique businesses fosters a sense of intimacy and connection that is difficult to achieve in larger settings. This close-knit environment allows for developing strong, lasting relationships between the firm, its clients, and its artists. These relationships are built on trust, mutual respect, and a deep understanding of each other's needs and goals.

This personal connection can be advantageous for clients and artists. It creates a supportive and collaborative atmosphere where their voices are heard, their ideas are valued, and their contributions are recognized. This sense of partnership and community is often missing in the impersonal, profit-driven world of large corporations.

NICHE EXPERTISE: MASTERY IN SPECIFIC AREAS

Boutique businesses discover niche markets by focusing on specific genres, styles, or services. This specialization allows them to develop a deep understanding and mastery of their chosen area, offering expertise unrivaled by larger, more generalized companies.

Take, for example, a boutique music production company specializing in a particular music genre. The company's intimate knowledge of that genre enables it to provide exceptional production services that capture the essence and nuances of the style. The boutique firm's expertise can be a game-changer for artists seeking to create music within that genre, helping them achieve a sound that might be unattainable elsewhere.

QUALITY OVER QUANTITY: THE BOUTIQUE COMMITMENT

The mantra of boutique businesses is clear: quality over quantity. These firms prioritize excellence in every project they undertake, ensuring that each receives the attention and resources needed to succeed. This meticulous approach often results in superior products and services that stand out in a crowded marketplace.

Whether it's a meticulously produced album, a flawlessly executed event, or a carefully curated talent roster, the boutique business's commitment to quality is evident in every aspect of its aspirations. This dedication to excellence can particularly appeal to clients and artists unwilling to compromise on their vision and standards.

CULTIVATING COMMUNITY AND CULTURE

Boutique businesses often cultivate a strong sense of community and culture within their company and with their audience. Creating a loyal fan base and a supportive network that champions their work. The culture within a boutique firm is typically one of collaboration, creativity, and passion, attracting like-minded individuals who share a commitment to excellence and innovation.

COST EFFICIENCY: VALUE WITHOUT COMPROMISE

Despite their high standards, boutique businesses offer competitive pricing due to lower overhead costs. They can allocate their budget more efficiently, focusing on delivering exceptional value without the excesses and inefficiencies plaguing larger corporations. This cost efficiency allows boutique firms to provide better value for money, making their high-quality services accessible to a broader range of clients.

EXCLUSIVE OPPORTUNITIES AND UNIQUE EXPERIENCES

Working with a boutique business can provide clients and artists with exclusive opportunities and unique experiences that might be lost in the vast machinery of a large corporation. The close relationships, personalized attention, and creative freedom offered by boutique firms can lead to truly unique collaborations and projects.

CONCLUSION: THE BOUTIQUE BUSINESS AS A BEACON OF EXCELLENCE

In a world where faceless giants appear to dominate the music and entertainment industry, boutique businesses stand as beacons of excellence, creativity, and personalized service. Their ability to offer tailored experiences, adapt quickly, and maintain close relationships with clients and artists sets them apart, making them an attractive option for those seeking more than just a business transaction.

The boutique business model proves that bigger is not always better in music and entertainment. By focusing on quality, creativity, and personalized service, boutique firms provide a refreshing and valuable alternative that enriches the industry and elevates the experiences of those they serve.

Once I realized that people viewed being independent as a bootstrapper's only approach, I wanted to reposition how I categorize our business. We are boutique, not indie. That starts to change how you view things because when you think of Boutique, it makes you feel more high-end and specific. It is a more personalized model for the direct needs of customers who want the service. In music, the service is very cookie-cutter. There is no long-term planning.

Chapter 9

DON'T GET SUNBURNED

"Let each of you look not only to his own interests, but also to the interests of others."

— Philippians 2:4

When the spotlight hits, it's easy to forget how you got there. The shine can make you think it's all about you, that you're untouchable, and that every move you make is the right one. But here's the truth: nothing burns faster than unchecked ego under the heat of success. "Don't get sunburn" is more than a warning—it's a call to check yourself, stay human, and remember that success is as much about the people you lift up as it is about your achievements.

THE GLOW CAN BLIND YOU

Success feels good. It's addictive, even. The calls are constant, the invites exclusive, and the opportunities endless. But here's what they don't tell you: the glow of success can blind you to the humanity of others. It's subtle at first. You're busy, so you skip a call back. You've become so focused on the next big thing so you forget to thank someone for their help. Then one day, you look up and a wall has been built between yourself and those who supported you the most. That's when the sunburn starts.

When caught up in the heat, you can start treating relationships as transactions—what can they do for me? That's not support, that's extraction. It leaves people feeling used, unvalued, and burned. And here's the catch: the

39

ones you take for granted today are the ones you'll need tomorrow. Bridges burned in the heat of success can't be rebuilt when the flame dies down.

THE COST OF FORGETTING YOUR ROOTS

Success often creates distance, not just physically but emotionally. You start moving in new circles, building new connections, and you forget about the people there before the glow-up. Maybe it's not intentional, but intent doesn't erase the impact. What happens when the people who loved you for who you were, not what you had, no longer feel welcome? What happens when your circle becomes a reflection of what you've gained instead of who you are?

Here's the thing: success is fleeting. The same people hyping you up today might not be there tomorrow. But the people who genuinely care about you supported you without expecting anything in return? They're rare. They're valuable. And they deserve better than to be left behind because you got too close to the sun.

ARE YOU USING YOUR LIGHT OR ABUSING IT?

The sun is life-giving. It's powerful. But when misused, it burns. Think about the power you have when you're "hot." Are you using that light to nurture others, to help them grow, or are you scorching them with arrogance, neglect, or entitlement? Your success should be a source of warmth, not destruction.

Think about the people who cross your path. The assistant who works overtime to keep your life organized. The young artist who looks up to you for guidance. The fans who pour their hearts into supporting your work. What do they feel when they interact with you? Do they leave better than they came, or do they feel drained, unseen, and undervalued?

Success isn't just about what you achieve; it's about how you make others feel. If you're not intentional, you risk becoming the very thing you once despised—a taker in a world full of givers.

THE SPIRITUAL WEIGHT OF LIFTING OTHERS

Building people isn't easy, but it's necessary. It's spiritual work. Every time you pour into someone else, you invest in something bigger than yourself. And let's be clear: it's not about being a savior. It's about being a supporter.

It's about recognizing the value in others and doing what you can to help them realize it.

I don't want you to think this means giving handouts or doing the work for them. It means creating opportunities, sharing knowledge, and being a resource when it matters. It means being the kind of person who people look at and think, "Because of them, I didn't give up."

Success isn't just about climbing the ladder—it's about pulling others up with you. Because when you reach the top, it's lonely without the people who matter.

THE LONG SHADOW OF SUCCESS

How you treat people when you're up casts a long shadow. It defines your legacy. Will people remember you as someone who used their power for good, or will they talk about how you let the shine change you? Will they remember the warmth of your support, or the sting of being burned?

Here's the reality: the same sun that warms also burns. The same light that draws people in can push them away if you're not careful. It's all in how you choose to use it.

When you're "hot," it's easy to think the glow will last forever. But it won't. Fame fades. Trends change. The calls stop. And when the heat cools, all that's left is your character. Did you use your time in the sun to build something lasting, or did you let the heat consume you?

PRACTICAL WAYS TO STAY GROUNDED

1. **Stay Humble**: No matter how big you get, remember where you started. Remember the people who believed in you when you were just a dream.
2. **Give Back**: Use your resources to create opportunities for others. Whether it's mentorship, donations, or just showing up for someone, make it count.
3. **Check Your Ego**: Success isn't a license to treat people poorly. Keep your ego in check and stay approachable.
4. **Be Intentional**: Every interaction is an opportunity to leave someone better than you found them. Don't waste it.
5. **Remember the Future**: Today's success doesn't guarantee tomorrow's. Invest in relationships that will last beyond the heat of the moment.

Final Reflections

"Don't get sunburn" is more than advice—it's a mindset. It's about staying grounded, staying human, and using your light to build, not burn. It's a reminder that success is only as meaningful as the lives it touches.

So, as you navigate your journey, remember Philippians 2:4. Look beyond yourself. Support others. Let your light be a blessing, not a burden. Because at the end of the day, your legacy isn't what you achieve—it's the people you uplift along the way.

Chapter 10
FINANCIAL LITERACY IS THE NEW SEXYY RED

When building a business, especially in the music industry, bad financial practices are often the norm. From excessive spending on unnecessary products to predatory contracts, the pitfalls are everywhere. But financial literacy can change the game entirely—it's not just practical, it's essential. This chapter will explore how financial literacy impacts the music business, personal growth, and long-term success.

The music industry often mirrors other predatory financial systems. For instance, new artists are advanced large sums of money—seemingly a blessing —but the reality is a different story. These advances, paired with high royalty rates and 100% recoupable costs, turn into loans with steep interest rates.

Imagine receiving $550,000 to create an album. If your royalty rate is 20%, you'll need $2.5 million in revenue to recoup that advance. Add producer payouts from your share, and the math becomes daunting. This cycle of debt is no different than payday loans or bad credit deals targeting college students.

Changing the Narrative means making Smart Deals. Financial literacy empowers artists to negotiate better deals. Consider demanding an 80% royalty instead of 20%, accepting a smaller advance, and minimizing unnecessary costs. Living below your means is key to scaling your business. By reducing initial debt, artists retain more of their earnings and avoid the endless cycle of dependency.

An example: By pushing labels to cover 50% of marketing costs, you not only reduce your debt but also incentivize greater label investment in your success.

LEARNING THROUGH EXPERIENCE

From balancing books for tours to understanding P&Ls (Profit and Loss statements), real-world experience was a critical teacher for COLTURE. By 2018, our team was operating entirely on cash and personal credit, without the safety net of label funding. Each payment, plan, and hire had to be intentional and strategic.

For example, when planning tours, announcing dates early allowed us to generate revenue from music sales and avoid the need for loans. Forecasting and financial foresight were essential.

By 2018, with the help of professionals, including my cousin, who is an accountant with over a decade of experience working at The Wall Street Journal / Dow Jones, we developed a simple but sophisticated financial system for an indie/boutique company. From forecasting growth to creating P&Ls, these tools were instrumental in scaling our business.

Today, templates and resources online make these systems accessible to everyone. Financial literacy isn't just about knowing math; it's about understanding systems like balance sheets, credit facilities, and growth projections.

THE REAL KEY TO INDUSTRY SURVIVAL

The Key to Independence is pace. Independence often means moving at the pace of your finances. Without external funding, we learned to bootstrap creatively: hiring consultants part-time, trading equity or royalties, and prioritizing essential investments.

Our journey wasn't without challenges. Trusting industry experts was difficult, so we declined offers to sell early equity. Staying independent allowed us to align our finances with our long-term vision.

Understanding money changes everything. When you know the value of a dollar and how to retain it, you negotiate smarter, build more sustainable systems, and create lasting success. Financial literacy isn't just sexy—it's the key to thriving in any industry.

Chapter 11

THESE CONVERSATIONS DON'T COME CHEAP

Let me be real with you: In this game, everything starts with the right conversations. When you're an independent company operating outside the major system, you have to build your own ecosystem brick by brick. And the foundation? Conversations. Because conversations lead to information, information leads to progression, and progression always finds the money trail.

Always.

Without the proper information, even when you touch the bag, you won't know what to do with it. Or worse, you'll fumble it and end up backtracking on your goals. So when we talk about "These Conversations Don't Come Cheap," we're not just talking dollars—we're talking value, integrity, access, and time.

PAYING TO PLAY

When we set up Lost Kids, we didn't want to follow the major label playbook. We wanted something real, sustainable, and ours. We weren't just paying producers a fair rate—we were cutting checks that had them eating off gross royalties, not net. Net is a whole different beast.

Gross means they're eating before the artist, before the label, before taxes hit. And we weren't stopping there. Songwriters? Same deal—they were part of the master royalty split. That's unheard of in the industry, but it's what we knew was right.

Now, let's talk global game. Building a team internationally isn't for the faint of heart or light of wallet. It takes real bread and vision. For instance, we didn't just hire a radio team; we incentivized them. They got 1-3% of the gross revenue from radio records. That's not cheap, but it's effective. They weren't just employees—they were stakeholders.

BUILDING THE TRIBE

You can't build an empire with just money; you need a tribe of like-minded people who value what you value. Mentorship, partnerships, and alliances are all key pieces. And don't get it twisted—those don't come cheap either. Mentorship? It takes effort, persistence, and humility. Partnerships? You have to show up with value, not just expectations.

In summer 2018, we put $70,000 into a national radio campaign for a Brent record called "Gang Over Luv." For perspective, that's a low number when you're competing for the #1 spot in the U.S. market for urban radio charts. But we were in the trenches, building infrastructure, hiring staff to run daily ads, and learning the ropes of digital impressions. You don't even know why that's important until you've had the right conversation with the right person who puts you on game.

THE COST OF INTEGRITY

Sometimes the most expensive conversations aren't about money. They're about keeping your word, even when it hurts. They're about taking losses so others can win because you understand the long game. This industry is built on relationships, and trust is your currency. You can't put a price on honor and integrity, but let me tell you, the lack of it? That'll cost you more than you're ready to pay.

We worked with Human Re Sources, who took 20% of our business for certain releases. If we made a million off a project, $200,000 went to them. Was it expensive? Hell yeah. But was it worth it? Absolutely. They brought value we couldn't buy anywhere else, and even today, their impact on our business is undeniable.

THE MANAGER'S ROLE

Let's be clear: The manager isn't just a glorified assistant. A real manager is the backbone of an artist's career. They need to see around corners, ask the tough questions, and make moves that protect both the artist and the business. They're the ones who turn potential into progress, and they do it while balancing trust, strategy, and execution. Artists depend on managers to avoid the traps this industry sets at every turn.

THE PRICE OF KNOWLEDGE

Every piece of information you gain in this business comes with a cost. Sometimes it's money. Sometimes it's time. Sometimes it's swallowing your pride and admitting you don't know everything. And sometimes, it's about paying it forward to those who need mentorship, just like you did.

The bottom line? These conversations are never cheap, but they're always worth it. The right conversations will build your infrastructure, strengthen your tribe, and set you apart in a world full of shortcuts and scams. So, what's the price you're willing to pay to grow?

By January 2020, I had invested heavily in my education. I had enrolled in an online master's program in sports management, traveled to different cities for business and entertainment conferences, and even purchased season tickets for basketball and football games to give as gifts to those who had helped me along the way. I made it a point to personally invest the most in my business, my education, and my community.

I was willing to do whatever it took to gain knowledge that would help me grow. I hadn't fully realized before that not coming from money also meant missing out on the information and opportunities that often comes with it.

Chapter 12

DIVERSIFY THE HUSTLE

By now, you're deep into the Playbook, and you should be ready to move past the basics and start stacking multiple hustles. The way the game works, you can't just focus on one bag; you gotta spread your wings, expand your reach, and make sure your money's coming in from different angles. You dig?

Now, let's keep it real. You can't just throw stuff at the wall and hope it sticks. You need to be strategic. Diversifying your hustle isn't just about jumping into whatever's hot. It's about using the foundation you've already built and expanding smartly. That means leveraging the skills you've developed in one hustle and taking them to other industries. Let's break it down.

GET EDUCATED, THEN MAKE MOVES

When we first started diversifying, we didn't go all in on everything at once. It was all about strategy, patience, and education. For me, it started with the music game. We built out Lost Kids, brought Amber Olivier into the fold, and started the Sonder band business, Sonder Global—each of these businesses playing off the music hustle we had already perfected. But that wasn't enough. You can't just stay stuck in one lane, I mean, you can, but that isn't what we decided to do.

I got into stocks, specifically marijuana stocks. These weren't major investments yet, but I knew the game wasn't about making moves just for the short term. It was about planting seeds for the future. So, yeah, we threw a little money into crypto, too—a small bet with a long-term outlook. The key here is patience, fam. Investments take time to pay off, so don't get

49

discouraged if things don't blow up overnight.

TRANSFERABLE SKILLS = THE KEY TO MULTIPLE HUSTLES

The most underrated thing in business is transferable skills. This ain't just about having expertise in one field; it's about taking that knowledge and applying it to other ventures. Music taught me project management, budgeting, and dealing with people at every level of the business. Those skills aren't exclusive to the music industry—they translate to anything.

For example, I learned a ton about organizing assets. The basics of building a project management system for music rights are transferable to any business. You might be running a record label or flipping real estate, but knowing how to manage your resources is a game-changer no matter where you are. The same goes for building relationships—whether pitching songs, products, or partnerships, the principles of selling are universal.

But don't get it twisted—just because you're great at one thing doesn't mean you'll automatically kill it in another.

You gotta understand the nuances of every hustle you dive into. It's not just about what you know, but about learning the language of each game.

PLAN YOUR MOVES, DON'T RUSH IT

Before you start branching out, you've gotta make sure your main hustle is stable. That's your foundation, right? If you're jumping into something new while your first hustle is on shaky ground, you're just spreading yourself too thin. Diversifying takes time—it's a balancing act. You don't just dive into a new hustle because it looks good on paper. You study it, plan it, and make sure you have the bandwidth to execute.

For me, that meant getting certified to represent NBA players, even though I didn't have the NFL certification yet. I studied for three years before taking the test to obtain my certification, and then I started working on expanding into sports. I didn't just take the first opportunity that came my way. I studied the market, did the groundwork, and then made my move. That's how you diversify smart.

MULTIPLE HUSTLES = LESS RISK

One thing you don't wanna do is put all your eggs in one basket. Diversifying helps reduce your risk. If all your income is tied to one thing—let's say, just managing music artists—then you're putting yourself in a position where if that hustle falters, you're stuck. By having multiple streams, you're insulating yourself from that risk.

You want money coming from different places: management deals, record labels, publishing rights, investments in things like real estate or tech. We even expanded into publishing with Cowboys and Pirates, a publishing company we built on the side. That wasn't just about music—it was about creating another revenue stream.

The key? You're not abandoning your first hustle. You're just ensuring that when the pressure comes from one side, you have other bags waiting to catch it.

KNOW WHEN TO LET YOUR TEAM IN

Don't keep everything to yourself. Let your partners know when you're making moves in new directions. Diversifying isn't about keeping secrets; it's about building transparency. They should understand the bigger picture and why you're branching out. It's not about taking focus away from your main hustle, but about using your wins to fuel other projects.

Sometimes, you can even involve your team. If it makes sense, let them participate in the new ventures. But always keep communication open and ensure they understand your vision. Everyone needs to be aligned so no one feels blindsided.

KEEP IT SMART, KEEP IT PLAYER, KEEP IT PRAYER

At the end of the day, diversifying your hustle is about being smart. You're building a legacy—not just a momentary win. Use your skills, take educated risks, and invest in what you believe in. The hustle isn't just about working harder; it's about working smarter, knowing when to take a step back, and when to step up. Play the long game, and keep it player.

And remember, diversification isn't about making 50 different moves at once. It's about picking the right opportunities that align with what you're already good at. Master one thing, then move on to the next. And trust me, once you start stacking those hustles, you'll see the magic happen.
Stay sharp, stay hungry, and keep building your empire. That's the hustle. Keep it real.

Chapter 13

FUCK YOU MONEY IN THE SUMMERTIME

The summers of 2018 and 2019 all felt like Fuck You Money Summers (this statement feels like some premium street wear merchandise). Let me explain more in depth and break it down summer by summer.

Let's dive into two pivotal summers that shaped our journey: 2018 and 2019. These were the "Fuck You Money" summers that redefined our path.

SUMMER 2018: LAYING THE GROUNDWORK

2018 was the first summer I wasn't juggling a job at Delta Air Lines. We had a major investment decision on the table, and regardless of the outcome, I had to leave Delta. I promised myself I'd stick with Delta only as long as it didn't hinder us from making money. By summer 2018, we wrapped up the first leg of Brent's headline tour, hit Europe for the second leg, and were gearing up for the third leg, targeting smaller B and C markets—about 13 to 14 shows. These smaller venues were crucial for building long-term fans.

By this time, I'd brought on Jayne as a co-founder. We were grinding daily, planning, building systems, and wearing multiple hats. The challenge was that while Jayne identified areas needing attention, we lacked the manpower to tackle them due to our management duties. If you're in management, you know how consuming it can be.

In 2017, we generated around $500,000 to $600,000, reinvesting almost 90% back into the business. Starting in 2018, we came in hot, making nearly $300,000 in the first quarter, on track to surpass the previous year's

53

performance. That summer, we solidified our audience with over 30 + shows across 36-37 U.S. cities, each with an average of 250-capacity venues, confirming a real core fan base.

Our ventures were expanding: Sonder's business was growing, Brent's brand was elevating, and our investment in Amber Olivier was progressing. At the time, we had a strong partnership with Human Re Sources. Brent was working on his second EP, Lost, and taking unprecedented control over his creativity. This shift allowed me to focus more on the business side, building the infrastructure for Lost Kids, which was COLTURE—"Can Our Leverage Teach Us Real Equity?"

We used Lost Kids as a prototype to showcase how our infrastructure worked. We generated enough revenue to cover bills and operate without being broke or needing side jobs. We were still sharing cribs, but by summer 2018, we were figuring out how to get our own spots. Being on tour meant we didn't need multiple places.

We finished 2018 strong, using the summer to plan for the fourth and first quarters of 2019. Our summers are planned meticulously to set up the rest of the year. We built strategies around Brent's Lost EP, deciding on video shoots and other creative aspects. We doubled down on the U.S. market, strengthening our systems—operational agreements, project management tools, payroll systems, taxes, and 1099s. Summer 2018 was about getting all these in order and aligning our partnerships.

SUMMER 2019: EMBRACING FULL INDEPENDENCE

2019 was the summer of full-blown independence. We'd wrapped up our first successful tour and planned the second one. Brent collaborated with The-Dream in early 2019, which revolutionized his songwriting approach. My focus was on growing the business internationally. We invested heavily in Europe—London and Paris—for fashion purposes and to expand Brent's international audience.

Brent introduced me to a track called "Fuck the World," he was extremely excited about it and wanted to release it ASAP. We crafted a marketing plan around "Fuck the World: Summer in London," followed by "Rehab: Winter in Paris." We intentionally included city names in the song titles to target growth in those areas.

We spent time in London, building internationally, especially in Europe—

France, the UK—shooting videos, collaborating, hosting events, and creating art. That run birthed the "Fuck the World" project, which significantly impacted our lives.

By July 2019, we were set on the "Fuck the World" project and planned a tour with bigger markets. Summer 2019 was the "Fuck You Money" summer. In 2018, we built the infrastructure; by 2019, we had the financial freedom to grow our business without relying on a record label. We just needed to move right and execute properly.

These two summers were crucial in growing our business, building an international presence, and ensuring we never had to work for anyone else again. That's the essence of the "Fuck You Money" summers.

THE "CREW" EFFECT: A RETROSPECTIVE PT. 2

Y: You guys weren't trying to take advantage of "Crew" with all the attention around it.

T: Nah, I didn't want that to be his moment 'cause it wouldn't have been true, plus, we didn't own the record.

Y: So many people have associated "Crew" with him though.

T: One hundred percent. But I think, if we had taken that moment, we would have signed a record deal. Cause RCA was on us hard.

Y: They were on you after "Crew" came out?

T: They were on us early, just as an A&R fan. But when that record dropped and it started growing, RCA was trying to get as much of the record as they could from an artist's perspective.

Y: I guess you really did fall into independence just by understanding what you didn't want.

T: If any label would have told me, 50-50, joint venture profit share, I would have signed it, bro. I would have thought that was fair at that time. I ain't giving a motherfucker 50% today. That's a wrap.

Y: I guess there's no deal you would take for Brent right now, is it?

T: Hell no. The only deal we will take with Brent right now is a film deal, a movie deal. We'll go to Paramount or Amazon Prime. We're off record deals. Record deals don't matter because we know what we got to do and we have several revenue streams to pull money down from unconventional loan partners so we can go out and build departments in different countries, or we can hire small teams in other countries on retainer to work on our behalf. That's no different than staff journalists. I can go out and hire a bunch of staff companies to work on our behalf in the markets that we don't understand, but they understand.

Y: I feel like if you would have signed a record deal we wouldn't be having this conversation.

T: No, I would have been in the system trying to figure it out and being frustrated. I know I'd be frustrated because I've represented clients that's in the system but not in the Colture community and that frustrated me.

Y: That system is not changing.

T: Nah, it's not changing. They made too much money off that motherfucker man. They're not going to change until they see that they're going to go broke or it's not going to work anymore. Right now, current day, it's still working. They're still signing record deals. People are still signing record deals. They're not going to change until people stop signing the deals that they put in front of them. Then they would think about changing it or alternating it.

I'm not just saying this for big artists, like Brent. I am 1000% speaking up for the artists who don't have a presence but have great ideas, they should get a fair deal. They should get a 50-50 profit split deal. That should be the only deal that an artist is taking at a major label. If they want to negotiate their master ownership or position themselves so they can buy their master's back and it's decided in the deal early, cool. But when it comes to paying them, there shouldn't be any deal but a net profit split.

Y: That's for any artist?

T: That's for any artist, I don't care how big or small he is – unknown or known. If you're known, obviously you can get better leverage. But baseline, you should be walking in any conversation as a 50-50 split partner.

Y: Heard you.

T: This is what people fail to realize; I was being independent by myself. What I mean by that is, Brent wasn't on that same wave as me. He didn't really care. When somebody don't care, they can swing either way. Several times I had to talk him out of signing a record deal several times, because, as an artist, you can look at people, your peers, and you can see your peers growing fast and you're like, man, my stuff is more competitive than theirs, my quality is better than theirs, I sound better, so why ain't I moving faster?

The answer to that is, usually, to sign a record deal and that was never my answer. My answer was always let's do better planning. Let's open up our minds to more unique ideas. Now he understands, he's lock and step with me now when it comes to this independence shit. So now, when I'm going to raise capital, venture capitalist money for Colture, I'm raising it because I know that the breadwinner is an equity partner, not only 50-50 in his company that he started, but he's also going to be an equity partner in this overall community that we're building.

Y: When did he start getting it?

T: When the pandemic hit.

Y: Y'all business wasn't affected how everybody else business was?

T: Not at all.

Y: I think that is a key component here, because, you can't plan a pandemic, but you can plan the infrastructure for your business.

T: You definitely can.

Y: I don't know if you've been keeping up with the Verzuz matches, but Erykah Badu, in her Verzuz, said that her business was built on touring. When touring stopped, her business changed, and I feel like that's the industry. Everyone's business is built on touring.

T: 100%

Y: No one really knew how to build their business any other way. All artists are taught is how to sign to a label and hit the road. So what made you not build Brent's business, or Wintertime's business, around touring?

T: One, because Brent didn't really like touring. You don't build no shit around... This is why COLTURE is going to be groundbreaking when it's launched properly. It's because we build the business around who the artist is. And at the time, this particular artist did not like touring. So why would I build some shit that a nigga don't like doing? We just had to scale our business based on how the music grows off music sales, publishing earnings, and when we launch our merchandise business.

When an artist likes recording music, putting music out, selling merch, that's what he loves, so I'm gonna build a business around that. So that way he doesn't have to go out on the road if he don't want to and when he does go out on the road, he's going to see a spike in his business. And if there's a nigga that wants to go on the road like a motherfucker, then we can plan a percentage of his business to be stimulated by him being out on the road.

Y: Okay, let's say you have an artist who doesn't want to go on the road. You're not trying to figure out a way to get that to happen? I mean, obviously, when you're brand new, how are people supposed to see you? How do you rectify that?

T: Well, for him, what we did was, we toured when we needed to tour to market a body of work. So we have the off-season and season. During the season, we're going to tour for 12 months and in that 12 months, we're going to do all the gigs that make sense. But when he's off-season, he's off-season. I don't give a fuck who's calling. He's off-season at this point.

Y: So he never felt forced, like he had to do something?

T: Nah, I mean, it was a little bit of, yo, we have to do this to grow. It was a little of that, but it wasn't going to be a thing where, if you don't do this, you ain't going to make no money.

Y: I feel that tends to be the mentality: You don't do this, you don't make money.

T: 100%

Y: For you to say you're building businesses around the artist, usually, I feel the business is already built and the artists are inserting themselves into the business, not vice versa.

T: Yes and no. They are building the business around the artist, but, the way they put the perception around it, they take everything from the artist like a work-for-hire. So they're building a business around owning the masters. That's how the circulation of the money is even in flow. Whoever owns it, controls the bulk of the money. They can't own touring. That's why the artists empower themselves through touring because nobody truly owns their touring.

Yeah, they can do a deal with Live Nation or a deal with AEG that will say, okay, we'll give you half a million dollars for two tours. You're like, okay, cool, I'm going to go on two tours. I got half a million dollars that they gave me upfront. Then on the back end, I got to pay them a percentage of this. Then once I'm recouped, I pay them a percentage of this until I'm out of this deal.

But, in essence, nobody can't force you to go on the road, they just have that debt. The only way you can produce a show is if you're tangible, in real life, on that stage. But once you turn a song in, a person can take that song, remix that song, and make it work in so many different ways.

Y: So tell me this, in today's time, what do you need to operate as an independent label?

T: An experienced team, or a team willing to learn. Having an artist who understands the patience that it's going to take to keep growing your business year over year. And having really solid relationships. Then I think the content plays a part in how big you gonna be. I don't think the content plays a part in how successful. You can be big and independent or you can have a business that takes care of your family in a way that's considered successful.

Y: Where do you think, in this day and age, most recording artist will make their first real income?

T: If I'm a new artist and I got all this information, I'm going to focus on my music catalog and pitching for sync. I would focus on out of the gate as your No.1 and No.2. Because touring costs money and it's not as profitable in the early days. Sync and putting out music are your most low-cost development of products that don't require you to hire many people. I would double down and do all the research needed to know how to build a catalog and pitch for syncs. Because syncs don't matter how big of an artist you are, you get ten syncs at $1,000, that's $10,000 and you still own your music and all you have to do is learn that business.

Y: When did you start learning the sync business?

Ty: I would say 2017. That's when I started to understand it like, oh shit, this is some real money. You can drive your entire business off this shit. You can have a million dollars in sync and only make $100,000 off music sales from a streaming perspective. Sync is a part of the income from your music, you just have to have a song work in that world.

Y: What happened in 2017?

Ty: Goldlink's "Crew" and Sonder's "Too Fast." Well, it was really 2016, with Wintertime's "Thru It All." He wrote and produced the entire record, but Erykah Badu did a cover. Issa Rae used it in Season 1, Episode 3 of Insecure. And being that it was a cover, we didn't get anything on the master recording side because it was a cover and they did some reworking on the production, but we got all the money on the publishing side.

Y: How did "Too Fast" get synced?

Ty: The first time it got synced was in the show Ballers. The crazy thing about it is, Scott Vener, known as Broken Mogul, placed it in Ballers. He's also responsible for getting Brent and Pharrell together.

Y: And "Crew?"

Ty: "Crew" was in Season 2, Episode 1 of Insecure. That set it off.

Y: So Wintertime and Brent both got syncs through Issa Rae's hit show.

Ty: We had Wintertime on Season 1. "Crew" in Season 2. I don't think we had anything in Season 3, but I helped Lil Simz get a placement in Season 3. We had one on Season 4 and we got something in the last season. So one of our clients can be heard on almost every season of Insecure.

Y: Those placements are all income that's not influenced by music streams or music sales?

Ty: Yep. One feeds the other. Gets synced and the record gets exposed. We also got a sync in the Netflix show My Block with a record Brent has called "Insecure." That spiked the record.

Y: What determines how much money each sync is worth?

Ty: Sometimes they're offering within the budget, and you can negotiate. Sometimes it's room to negotiate, sometimes it's not. You get more money on trailers, T.V. advertising campaigns, shit like that. Movie trailer a lot of money.

Way more money.

Y: Have you gotten a movie trailer?

Ty: Almost. Artists need to know syncs are a premium stream of income. It doesn't matter if you're signed to a record label or not. They prefer you not to be signed. The smaller number of people they have to talk to get it cleared is attractive to them. Like we had a sync, the Gap sync for Sonder, we were trying to get them to pay $500,000 for that sync, to use that song for one year. But you know, there was a lot of pushback and things like that, so we ended up settling at $250,000. Bro, $250,000 to use one song that has been out for over four years and we own the record. Collectively, we own, about, 60% of the publishing on that record. No, it was more like 70% of the publishing on that record.

So just think about all of the times you hear music on commercials during the NBA finals, and during the Super Bowl, that Black artists wrote, produced, but don't own. That's a huge business So when I say I see the other side of the curtain, my nigga, I see the other side of the curtain. I see what the labels see. You don't see what the label sees, and let them just give you... nah. That's why Russ went back independent.

Y: You're right, he didn't sign another deal.

T: You know why? Russ is hiring his own radio team. He's gonna go hire whatever, whoever, wherever he needs to, because, he understands, he sees what it is. He was in the system long enough to see what it was. Now he's going to hire the people he thinks can help him build his business better. That's how the labels are doing it. Now he has his own money to do it.

Y: But you never went into the system.

T: No, we are blessed. We're blessed man. I'm trying to take blessings and turn it into an operational thing. We were blessed to be able to see that code and crack it and not have to go through what he went through, even though his experience was probably positive or probably a little bit more positive than most. But he went in with leverage. So that's different.

Y: It is different.

T: He went in with a sold-out tour. All the labels were chasing him around, publishers were chasing him around. I remember it before he signed. For artists like him, artists like Young Dolph, like how DaBaby is starting to build his label

out. How Yo Gotti is starting to build his label out. Some of them are starting to really understand and see, like, wait a minute, I don't really need y'all how much I thought I did.

Y: Coming out of the pandemic, I wonder how artists are viewing what the label can do for them, and what they can do for themselves. And I guess what's fascinating about rap, is how street money can help fund it, but it's not just street artists who want to rap. So for someone who does not have any street money, and doesn't have any capital, how do they get into the game and get a fair shake?

T: They have to do just like any other fucking business owner had to do, they have to figure out how to bootstrap. Having good credit helps because you can run your business off your credit cards. Get a fucking job, so that you can invest in yourself. Listen, most artists are taken advantage of because they don't want to work. They want to work, but they don't want to work. There's a difference, a big-ass difference. So if you got a job, and you're spending 40 hours a week at your job, and you're spending 20 hours a week cutting your teeth trying to write the best records and you're saving your money and you're putting out one really great project a year and you're doing that for three years consistently with a team trying to help push you, you can't tell me that you won't increase your chances on getting away from that job by year four.

People sign to major labels because they give them the money so that they ain't got to go to that job, but really that job is really more helpful for them than they realize, not just from a financial perspective, but from a work ethic, obedience, discipline perspective.

Y: Well said. Year four does sound like the crossing of a threshold if you're able to get there.

T: May 2019 was the beginning of our fourth year.

Y: What do you think the most difficult year was for you guys?

T: The most difficult year? I would probably say 2016. I don't personally feel like any year was difficult. I've been having fun. It's hard to even spot difficulty.

Y: Yeah?

T: I can say, in 2016, January and February of that year, Brent was sleeping in my closet. I had a one-bedroom studio apartment that was less than 500 square feet. I didn't have any furniture but my bed. But we were able to go to the studio and record every single day.

Y: And that was fun?

T: Yeah, it was fun, because we were doing something we loved, we enjoyed.

Y: Did you think it was risky moving him in with you? This kid you found on SoundCloud?

T: By that time we had been dealing with each other for over a year. We met in August 2014. By the time he moved in with me, he had been chopping it up, talking, like, you should move to LA; don't move cold turkey, but let's try it out. It happened like that, but, like, most people would say, man, that's difficult, but we were just kids in the mud, having fun, recording every day. We could afford food. It was days when we didn't have money to do certain things, but we always could afford something to eat. We could always go back and forth home if we needed to go and reset because shit was a bit difficult. We could always afford flights. And we're doing music every day, every day we're going to the studio.

Y: That's amazing.

T: So I can say 2016 was difficult living circumstances, but I just always knew it was going to be work to get anything out of life that you're happy about.

Y: I don't know how you got wired like that, but it makes sense you guys landed where you are because of that mentality like, you weren't trying to take any shortcuts.

T: Nah, I never wanted to take shortcuts from the work, but I wanted my work to put me on a shorter route.

Y: That makes sense. Do you feel like you got a shorter route? I feel like your journey has been long.

T: I look at it from the standpoint of, like, everybody's journey is long. From them trying to figure out what they want to do, how they want to do it, all of those different things, right? I'm 36 years old. By the time I'm in my 40s, I've already cemented my legacy in the music business for our generation. So that's in four years. So the past four years and the next four years, that's eight years. So in eight years, I've already cemented what my legacy is going to mean in the music business. And I'll be 40.

I think my mom bought her first house… Let's see. My mom is 57. She bought her first house in the summer of 2003. So that was 17 years ago. So my mom purchased her first house right before she turned 41. Making $40,000 a year.

Y: What does she do now?

T: Nothing. She's retired. And she ain't gonna do nothing as long as I'm alive.

Y: Heard that.

T: So, for me, the journey was nothing but me living life and learning and experiencing. But if any of us can make an impact on this world before we turn 40, we done cut the shortcut, especially being black. And I'm talking about a real impact. I'm not talking about, like, a platinum-selling record, I'm talking about a real impact where you change the dynamic of how business is being done, how people view the business.

Y: That's not superficial influence.

T: Yeah, it's bigger than just selling some records. So the thing about it is, when I sit down with other owners who have been business owners way longer than me, they see me in a different light than they see somebody else that's got a label deal at a record label where the record label owns all their records. My conversations are different and they're going to only keep being different because my ownership superpowers are going to keep growing.

Y: What do you want to be after 40? After you impact the entire business, after you build out Colture to be what it'll be, what's next for you?

T: By the time I'm 40, I'm going to be knee-deep into sports and film and commercial real estate, and of course, philanthropy is always going to be there.

Y: Why film? I get sports, that's your background. That's where you started, but what draws you to film?

T: Film gives me the ability to tell stories that I find to be interesting. Like, film is how I can be a recording artist. Like, I can write a song, but I can't go out and perform the song or be a songwriter, but I can put an idea together to write a film based on a story, no matter if it's something from my life, something from your life, something from my mother's life, and I can produce it. Record executive, sports agent, film executive, they all are synonymous through these stories, these unique stories that we see in our eyes and we tell them in different

ways. You know we're the best storytellers. Black people are the best storytellers. No matter what medium you want to put us on.

Colture Bonus

MANAGEMENT CHECKLIST

Vol. 2 Update

SIGNING

- Has the act been presented to the company and discussed internally?
- How is the negotiation of the management agreement being handled?
- Have you involved your team?
- Have you discussed the commission structure with your client? Has your client signed a written management agreement?
- Has your client had any team members before your involvement? (Manager, Booking Agent, PR Agent, etc)
- Is there a sunset agreement from a previous management? Do you have a copy of that?
- Have you asked your client directly if they have signed anything in the past? Do you have copies of any agreements?
- Does your client have any existing deals (record label, publishing, management, brand partnerships, etc...)?
- Does your client have an entertainment attorney?
- Does your client have an agent?
- Have you made sure your client's accounts are up to date?
- Have your artist's socials been reviewed by our digital marketing dept?
- Do you have logins for all of your artists' socials? Are there any channels that are missing?
- Does your client own any of their own media content that is being monetized?
- Does your client run all their digital properties on their own or do they

- utilize any outside agencies?
- Do you have passport scans for your client?
- Do you have your clients mailing address?
- Do you have your clients invoice details?
- Do you know what programs or instruments your client uses to make music?
- Do you have your clients clothing and shoe sizes?
- Do you have your clients legal documents (W-9, License scan, Passport scan)
- Are you aware of your clients financial status and their ability to support themselves through music?

REVENUE

PUBLISHING

- Do you know when your statements arrive?
- Have all works (new and old) been registered?
- Do you know the terms of your publishing deal? Splits, term, MDRC?
- Do you have to invoice your publisher for payment?
- Do you know the key dates to options and advances?
- Do payments go to business management, management or direct to the client?
- Do you know the key team members at this company, their function and how they can help you?
- Have you checked to make sure your artist's discography is up to date?

LABEL

- Do you know when your royalty statements arrive?
- Do you know the term of your deal and splits?
- Do you have to invoice your label for payment?
- Do you know the key dates to options and advances?
- Do payments go to business management, management or direct to the client?
- Do you know the key accounting team members at this company, their function and how they can help you?

SOUNDEXCHANGE

- Do you know when your royalty statements arrive?

- Have you double checked that the latest discography is up to date?
- Are you registered?
- Do payments go to business management, management or direct to the client?
- Do you know the key team members at this company, their function and how they can help you?
- Be aware that admin deals, neighboring rights collection service deals and distribution deals may ask to collect Sound Exchange monies on behalf of you and your artist for a percent of the earnings, try to negotiate this out of your deals as self-registration is very simple.

NEIGHBORING RIGHTS

- Do you have someone collecting Neighboring Rights for your performer, producer or label?
- Do you know who gets paid from neighboring rights?
- Do you understand neighboring rights?
- Do you know when your royalty statements arrive?
- Do payments go to business management, management or directly to the client?
- Do you know the key team members at this company, their function and how they can help you?
- Do you understand that incorrect label copy can affect your ability to collect neighboring rights?
- Are you aware of the countries where one can collect neighboring rights?
- Have you checked to make sure the discography is up to date/all titles are registered?

PERFORMING RIGHTS ORGANIZATIONS (ASCAP, BMI, SESAC IN THE US)

- Do you know when your royalty statements arrive?
- Do payments go to business management, management or direct to the client?
- Do you know the key team members at this company, their function and how they can help you?
- Do you understand how PRO's function and what money they collect on behalf of your artist?
- Do you have your artist's login information for these portals?
- Have you checked to make sure your artist's discography is up to date and that the performance and publishing side is registered?
- Are you in regular contact with a point person at your PRO?

- - Are they aware of you and your artist?
  - Have you reached out about potential collaborations?
- Is your client currently signed to any MCN (multi-channel network) agreements online?

BUSINESS MANAGEMENT

- Does your client have a business manager?
- If your client has a business manager, what is their fee structure?
- Are they a music business management company?
- Has your client filed taxes for their business every year?
- Do you have records of your client's tax filings for each year?
- Is your client registered as an LLC, S-Corp or Sole Proprietorship?
- Do you understand the difference in liability between the business structures above?
- Are you tracking and recording revenue for your artist on a regular basis? How often are you updating the artist revenue tracker? Are you automating revenue dashboards?
- Is your clients touring, recording and merch business as separate entities or one in the same?
- Do you understand the reason for having separate business entities for each of their revenue streams?
- Does your client have a "band agreement" in place should anyone leave or the act disbands?
- Does your client have a business credit card?
- Do you know all of your clients bank account information?
- Does your client have a line of credit with a bank?
- Do you have your clients wire transfer info?
- Do you have your clients W-9 (US) or W-8 (Europe) for payment purposes? Do you have a Federal Tax ID (US)? Do you have a VAT number (Europe)?
- Do you understand all of the areas your client receives revenue? (touring, music, publishing, merchandise, brand deals, syncs)
- Are you creating quarterly projections for your artists' earnings?

TOURING

- Does your artist have an LLC or Corp set up for touring income?
- Is your business manager aware of the commission that needs to be paid to management on bookings?
- Are you aware of how much the agency is taking out of each fee for

- commission?
- How is the money being routed from the booking agency to your artist?
  - Direct to the artist?
  - Direct to business manager?
- How often do you receive statements from your booking agency?
- Are you cross-checking those statements with the touring calendar and show agreements?
- Are you creating show/production budgets for each show based on the fee and level of show importance?

BOOKING AGENT

- Who is your booking agent?
- What territories do they book?
- What are the terms with your booking agent?
- Are you aware of the teams at your booking agency?
  - Agent, assistant, finance, legal, etc.?
- What additional services are being offered by the booking agent?
  - Marketing, tour sponsorships, etc

GETTING STARTED

- Have you set up the master calendar that has been shared with the entire team?
- Have you set up the Master Revenue tracker for key team members to share?
- Have you added block dates to the Master Calendar (dates the artist can't tour - in the studio, vacation, family event etc...)?
- Have you or your artist's business manager set up tour insurance (N. America and Rest of World)?
- Have you asked your artist's business manager if your insurance covers all aspects (workers comp, specific touring equipment etc...)?
- Have you established a touring budget based on show fee and level of show importance?
- How often are you adding touring income to the revenue tracker?

TOURING CREW

- Have you hired a tour Manager (TM)?
- Have you hired a Production Manager?
- Have you hired a Lighting Director (LD)?
- Has your tour Crew signed personnel agreements?

- Are Payroll + Payroll taxes sorted for crew?
- Are you hiring a videographer or photographer?
- Is your videographer/photographer's equipment insured?
- Does anyone on the crew have a criminal record?
    - This can affect entry into some countries, Canada and Australia being strong examples.
- Does your crew need to apply for visas for international dates?**

*** Different for each country so check the moment an international show is booked. Some countries have a very difficult process. For Korea, Brazil, and the USA, a visa agent is strongly advised*

TRAVEL

- Will you use a travel agent?
- What is your artist's Frequent Flier #s for each airline alliance?
- What is your artist's Hotel Loyalty Program #s for each hotel alliance?
- What are your artist's Flight Preferences (aisle, exit row etc...)?
- What are your artist's Hotel Preferences (has a gym, late check out, etc...)?
- Has your artist registered for TSA pre-check and Global Entry?
- How are you tracking frequent flyer points/miles?
- Does your travel agent have all of the above information?
- Are you booking travel as soon as a run of shows are confirmed?
- How are you managing travel plans?
- Are you considering refundable vs. non-refundable tickets?
    - If non-refundable, how are you keeping track of flight credits for touring crew?

REVIEWING A SHOW OFFER

- How does it route with other shows in that date range?
- Will you be flying there?
    - If so, check flight schedules.
        - If commercial flights aren't available, consider a private jet if within budget
- Will you be driving there?
    - If so, check drive times, how much gear can fit into the vehicle, who on the crew has a driver's license, are they aware of all state driving laws?
- What is your guest list allocation and when is it due?
    - TIMING IS VERY IMPORTANT FOR FESTIVALS
- Who else is on the line-up and how many tickets can they sell in that

market?
- How will your artist be billed? (headline, second headline, support)
- What production elements will be made available to your artist?
  - To other artists on the bill?
- Can you pay for extra production elements?
  - (more confetti, more CO2, extra lights/lasers, bigger LED screens)
- Does taking this show affect relationships with other promoters in the region?
- How is the promoter connected to area festivals?
  - National festivals?
- What is the reputation of the promoter and venue?
- How does the money compare to previous plays in that market? In general?
- Who is supporting?
  - Are you getting approvals?
  - If a DJ, what style?
- If the show is a festival, can you sell merch and if so, how many items?
- What is the merch split with the venue?
- What is your artist's set length?
- Is there a back-end deal for this show?
- Do you know what 2 for 1 means?
- Do you know what landed deal means?
- Do you have a pre-sale allocation of tickets?
- Do you know what service you are using for presale?
- Has the promoter built in a marketing budget for the show?
  - How are they planning on allocating it?

IF BOOKED AS SUPPORT

- Is this audience the right one for your artist?
- What will your billing be?
- In what order will you play?
- How long is your set time compared to the other acts?
- What is your artist's guarantee each night?

ADVANCING PROCESS

- Have you confirmed advance contact and terms of the deal with the booking agency?
- Has the promoter signed off on the tech rider?
- Has the promoter signed off on the hospitality rider?
- Is the hospitality rider being taken out of your fee?

- Have you approved show art AND ad mat?
- Have you coordinated the show, announcement date, time, and ticket link with the venue/promoter?
- Have you or the TM sent travel plans to advance contact?
- Have you or the TM confirmed ground transport (airport > hotel, hotel > venue, venue > hotel, hotel > airport)?
- Have you or the TM confirmed set times and set order?
- Is this a union venue?
    - If so, get local union rules from the venue when advancing.
- What are the guest list allocations (Crew, AA, VIP, GA)?
- Are there any meet & greets or extra on-site activations that need to be planned around?

DAY OF SHOW SCHEDULE

- Load-In
- Perform Soundcheck before doors open
- Perform Visuals check before doors open
- Set up merch booth - confirm cash drawer, credit card machine, staffing, splits with venue, count in and count out each item
- Meet with security team Introduce yourself to everyone at FOH (front of house)
- Check guest list with the door and give them your cell # if there are questions/issues
- Re-confirm set times and set order - is enough time allotted for changeovers between acts?
- Collect Settlement (show and merch)

MARKETING

MUSIC RELEASE ASSETS

- Mastered WAV Files of Music
- Instrumental Files
- Lyrics
- Artist EPK
- Press Images
- Press Release
- Social Headers (YouTube, Facebook, Soundcloud, Twitter)
- Music Video

- Abbreviated Video Clips for Social Media
- PSD Files for all Logos and Art
- Release Art (at least 3000x3000)
- Writer Publishing Details and Splits / Signed Split Sheets
- ISRC Code for Release
- Remixes (if applicable)
- Release Timeline
- Release Marketing Plan
- Official Release Date from Label
- Signed Deal Memo from Label
- Newsletter

RELEASE PARTNERS

- Do you have relationships at key DSPs (Spotify, iTunes, Beatport, Pandora, etc.) ?
- What is the target audience for the track in terms of age and interests?
  - That can help determine what partners to reach out to and where to run any exclusives.
- Have you discussed features with key DSPs?
- Have you started finalizing the release schedule at least six weeks out to properly service all DSPs?
- Have you hired a PR agent to work your release?
- Are you aware of the key playlists (Spotify, Apple Music, etc.) that support your genre? Ex. Hot New Hip Hop, New Music Friday
- Have these playlists been made aware that you have a release coming?
- Have you been in touch with past playlists that have supported the artist?
  - You can find these through the Spotify Fan Insights portal under "playlists."
- Are there any online partners that can get involved in your tour or release?
- Are there any outside social influencers you can lock in to help spread awareness for the track?
- Do you have creator-safe music distribution in place for UGC usage?

TIMELINE

- Are you working towards a single album, EP, or other type of release?
- If you are releasing the song as an exclusive, how is the marketing ramping up for the exclusive release as opposed to the full release?
- Do you have a release schedule for the year or the next six months?
- If planning for a larger format release, what is your strategy for releasing

- music?
- Do you have a strategy to reach key blogs and garner their support for your release?
- What is your strategy to grow subscriber counts on specific streaming services?
- When will your press release go out? Who will service it?
- Are you securing premier partners to debut your release?
- Are you sending the release to key DJs to support ahead of release?
- Have you secured ad inventory on key web-sites?
- Are you letting fans know a release is coming ahead of release?
- Do you have social media assets to engage your fanbase? Ex. Video clips, GIFS, new images, live shots, etc.
- When will all digital properties (website, Facebook, Twitter, etc.) get updated with new creative around the release?
- Do you have a clear start and end date for working on this release?
- Have you reached out to past supporters to see if they can offer support for this release?
- Have you uploaded files to DSPs early enough to receive features (usually 4-6 weeks prior to release)
- What is the timeline for how paid digital spends will be allocated?
- Do you have a marketing strategy to keep people engaged with the music in the weeks/ months following the release?
- Do you have AI Integration checkpoints in place?

RADIO

- Have you hired a radio team to work your release?
- Does this team have success in your genre?
- Has this team worked with similar artists?
- Are you using MusicDNA or any other services to monitor broadcast airplay?
- Do you know what radio testing is and how it pertains to your radio campaign?
- Have you tested your song on radio?
- What score did your release receive from radio testing?
- When does your campaign start?
- When does your campaign end?
- Are you receiving weekly updates from your radio team?

VIDEO

1. Are your video files hi-res?

- Are your video files formatted for television and streaming platforms (MTV, Revolt, Apple Music, Tidal, etc.)?
- Are your video files mastered for iTunes?
- Have you hired a video promotions company to place your video with key outlets (MTV, Music Choice, Revolt) and secure plays of your video in physical retail spaces?
- How long is your video campaign?
- Are you receiving weekly updates from your video team?
- Is your artist properly set up with YouTube for Artists so you can track streams?
- Are you planning on exclusively debuting the video anywhere?
- If so, what is the guaranteed promotion they are providing?
- Is the video going on the artist's own YouTube page, or do you need to be using Vevo?
- Is all your metadata properly set up for wherever the video is living?
- Who is monetizing the video content? A specific MCN, the record label, the artist, or another entity?
- Are you putting up YouTube Cards on past videos directing fans to your newest one?

TOUR MARKETING

- Are you in touch with the marketing point person for each venue and or promoter?
- Does your agency have a dedicated marketing department that can be utilized?
- Have you requested marketing plans from all promoters?
- Does the promoter's marketing plan include radio ads and/or ticket giveaways, a local radio presenter, social media budget to promote the show online?
    - And how is the budget being allocated?
    - Street teaming outside of similar shows and other shows the promoter is putting on that can be used to promote your act
- Can you allocate some of the promoters online marketing budget to your socials?
- If there is a radio presenter?
    - Has your act recorded liners promoting the show and delivered them to the station?
- Is there the possibility for an in-studio interview when the artist is in town?
- Have you offered a mix from your artist for local stations?
- Has the promoter paid for billboards or snipes to promote your show?

- Has the promoter sent an email blast?
- Can the promoter provide you with an email blast you can send geo-targeted to the artist's email list?
  - If not, do you have a set email template you can use?
- Has the promoter pushed the show from their social outlets?
- How have the promoters of other shows with similar acts performed in the past?
  - Is it usually a walk-up crowd?
  - Are there specific audiences you should be targeting, etc.
- Has your act supported the show on social media?
- Have the other acts on the bill supported the show on social media?
- Have you created a tour announcement video to utilize in the press and through social media?
- Have you created video drops for each market on the tour?
  - Has this content been shared with promoters?
- Have you created a Facebook event for this show?
- Are you able to share with the promoter, so there is only one Facebook event around the show?
- Have you added the show to the artist's Bandpage, Bandsintown, Songkick, Thrillcall, Spotify, and any other artist sites?
- Are you messaging past attendees of shows in the area from old Bandsintown and Facebook events?
- What is your social media plan to promote this show or tour?
- Are you using a fan club, pre-sale, or VIP ticketing service that can help further promote your show?
- What's your budget for marketing this show or tour?

PAID ONLINE MARKETING

- Are you buying iAds through Apple to support your release on iTunes?
- Are you running any ads through Reddit?
- Are you running ads through Youtube to increase video views?
- Are you running banner ads on key online outlets?
- Are you running Meta ads?
  - How are they being run?
  - What is being done to optimize your ROI?
- Are you running any Snapchat custom filters around specific shows or events?
- Are you running ads through any ad networks?

EMAIL MARKETING

- Does your artist already have an existing email list?
- Where is the list being hosted?
- Do you have an email template made for new releases and major show or tour announcements?
- How has the artist been utilizing their email list in the past?
- Do you have a plan for consistent email communication going forward?

SOCIAL NETWORK/STREAMING

Does your artist have profiles on each of the following:
- Facebook
- Twitter/X
- YouTube
- SoundCloud
- Snapchat
- Instagram
- Reddit
- Apple Connect
- Tumblr
- TikTok
- Bluesky
- Threads (uses Instagram login)
- Bandpage
- Discord
- Kick
- Shazam
    - Has your artist been verified on Shazam?
    - Is there a schedule in place for pushing new music?

SPOTIFY

- Have you verified your artist profile and linked it with a personal Spotify account?
- Are you making playlists on the artist's official discography page and updating them regularly?
- Are you messaging those playlists fairly regularly?
- Are there any tracks missing from the artist's discography page?
- Are there any tracks on the artist's discography that have been mislabeled and need to be removed?

- Have you signed up for Fan Insights for Spotify for your artist?
- Have any major playlists supported your artist?
  - Are you in contact with those playlists?

SOUNDCLOUD

- Does your artist own any of the master recordings to songs on Soundcloud that they have full rights to monetize?
- Do you have Songkick added to your page, so tour dates are being pulled in?
- Do you have all the artists' digital networks added to the right-hand panel on the bio page?
- Is the first tag being used for all tracks the closest genre based on the genres on the Soundcloud "Charts" page?
- Is the artist willing to treat Soundcloud as a social network and interact with other users to create more conversation around their page?
- Is there information to buy/stream or host a gate-free download for all tracks in the metadata?
- Do you have a custom banner on the profile?
- Do you have the account upgraded to a Pro account?

INSTAGRAM

- Is your account verified?
  - Have you done the research to see if it looks like it may qualify?
- Do you have a link in your bio to direct to the artist's most current project?
- Are you using any third party apps to create richer photo/video assets?
  - Ex. Canva, Meitu, CapCut, InShot, etc.
- Are the posts providing value to the account?
- Is it content that your followers find useful or engaging but also reinforces your brand as well?
- Is the artist engaging their followers on a regular basis?
- Is the artist using hashtags consistently in the copy of their posts?
- Is the artist content with the username and display name?
  - Are you looking to change usernames?
- Do you know how to run Instagram ads, and are you actively running them?

FACEBOOK

- Is your page verified?

- o If not, have you done the research to see if it looks like it may qualify?
- Are you currently running any Facebook ads? Do you know how to run ads on Facebook?
- Are all the artist's digital properties added to the "About" page?
- Are you following current best practices for posting content (for instance, video usually performs exponentially better than other forms of media)?
- Are you creating dedicated Facebook events for ALL of the artist's upcoming live shows?
  - o Has the promoter been added to these?
- Does the page have a Bandsintown tab, and are you updating it as each new show is announced?
- Is the artist posting fairly regularly (at least every few days)?
- Does the page have separate tabs for Instagram, Twitter, Soundcloud, Youtube, and any other networks the artist is active on?
- Is the artist content with the username and display name?
  - o Are you looking to change usernames?
- Are you using high res video and photo content as much as possible?
- Do you have a content schedule, so there is consistent content in the near and far-term?
- Have you connected the artist's official Instagram page with Facebook so you can run ads concurrently on both?
- Do you have a channel trailer setup?
- Are you selling merch on the page?

TWITTER/X

- Is the page verified? If not, have you done the research to see if it looks like it may qualify?
- Is the artist posting content regularly and with an authentic voice?
- Do you have a profile banner setup?
- Is the artist uploading the video natively through the Twitter/X app?
- Are you consistently viewing the page stats through Twitter/X Analytics (https:// analytics.x.com/)?
- Do you have a "Community" on Twitter/X set up for fan based conversations and artist updates?
  - o Do you have someone that can be a moderator?

YOUTUBE

- Do you have a custom URL claimed for the artist's channel?
- Is there content being playlisted?
  - o Is there a channel trailer setup?

- Is the account verified, so you have the full suite of YouTube options?
- Is all of the artist's past discography either on their own YouTube or Vevo page?
- Is the page a YouTube Partner?
- Is it part of an MCN or monetizing any content?
- Have you checked all copyright claims on the page to ensure there is nothing that could hurt future uploads?

OTHER

- Is your artist verified on Shazam and constantly posting tracks on there?
- Do you have access to the artist's Apple Connect page?
- Do you have the artist's Google Plus page claimed and a bit of content on there, so it's on the Google Knowledge Graph?
- Does the artist have a Snapchat page claimed and continually posting content?
- Does the artist engage with UGC on social media platforms?

RELEASING MUSIC

RECORD DEAL

- Have you discussed these terms with senior members of staff and your attorney before agreeing?
- What are the terms of your deal?
- What are your deliverables?
- How does the label plan to recoup in advance (if any)?
- Are there different contracts for different territories?
- What is the label's marketing plan?
- How can your team supplement that plan?
- What is the label's marketing budget?
  - How are they planning on allocating that money?
- Are you aware of the roles and responsibilities of each person at the label?
  - Are you in touch with key team members?
- Have you spoken to the label's radio team?
- Are they doing radio testing on potential singles?
- Have you spoken with the label's sync team?
- Have you spoken with the label's digital team?
  - How invested are they going to be in your specific artist?
- Have you spoken with the label's branding/partnerships team?
- Who is your contact for label accounting?

- Have you organized and distributed a release plan to the team?

DELIVERABLES

- When will the cover art be ready?
- When will the music video be ready?
- Will there be any extra digital assets made to help promote the music?
- What is your release date?
- Are you making physical products?
- What is the deadline for CD printing?
- What is your asset delivery date to hit that release date?
- What is the deadline for vinyl pressing?
    - NOTE: THIS HAS A VERY LONG LEAD TIME
- Have you provided metadata for each track on the release?
- Do you have the ISRC for the release?
- Do you have the split sheet and signed release agreement?
- Do you have a final label copy?
    - Do you know how to format label copy properly?

REMIX PACKAGE

- Will there be a remix package?
- What is the budget for remixes?
- What is the delivery date for remixes?
- Who is remixing?
- What is the aim of each remix?
    - Territory, audience, marketing for remixes?
- Do remixers know to turn in final mixes, or have you allocated a budget for mixing and mastering?
- Have all remixers signed remix agreements?
- Do you have a set budget for marketing around the remixes?

RELEASING INDEPENDENTLY

- Are there other writers or artists on the release?
- Are deals in place with all artists and writers involved with the release?
- Have you set up accounting for those outside artists and writers?
- What digital distribution method are you using? Venice? Stem? United Masters?
- Do you have metadata for each track on the release?
- Will you send it out for licensing in other territories? If so, establish target labels & territories.

- Have you organized and distributed a release plan with the team?
- Have you talked about exclusives with various retailers?
- Are you set up to monetize the audio on YouTube and Soundcloud?
- Do you have specific thresholds you'd like to hit to call this a successful release? Ex. iTunes download, Spotify streams, YouTube plays, Soundcloud streams, etc
- Do you have short-form content on standby to release? Monetizable? (IG Reels, TikTok, Shorts)

PRODUCTION

- Is there a sample used?
  - Has it been cleared?
- Who is mixing?
- Who is mastering?
- Do you have a budget for this release to cover creative costs?
- Do the tracks need to be mixed and mastered for specific formats?
  - i.e. iTunes and vinyl
- Do you have the mastered stems?

RADIO SHOW

- Does your artist already have an established radio show or mix series?
  - Is it being syndicated on radio in any territory?
- Is it live in iTunes Podcasts?
  - Do you have control over the server where the audio is hosted?
  - Are you running any analytics on where the downloads are coming from?
- Are you posting the audio to SoundCloud, YouTube, and other streaming outlets?
- Are you utilizing guest mixes in the radio show?
- Do you have a specific photo and video assets made for each new episode?

PRESS

GETTING STARTED

- Who is your artist's PR agent?
- Does your artist have different PR agents for different territories?
- Is the PR agent affiliated with your label?
- Who covers the cost of PR? Your artist or the label?

CREATE EPK (ELECTRONIC PRESS KIT - CONTAINS THE FOLLOWING)

- Artist Bio
- Press Shots (headshot, full-body, personality shots)
- Hi-Res Artist Logo
- Branding Guide (Design details on your logos, texts/typeface to be used along with your assets, color direction, etc.)
- Document with links to all Artist socials & web properties
- Press clippings
- Quotes from key press outlets
- What's the overall fan sentiment online for the artist? Ranker (http://www.ranker.com/) can be an excellent resource for this.

ONGOING

- Are you saving all past press releases to a central shared location?
- Are you keeping all past press clippings to a central shared location?
- Do you have a list of all press contacts?
- Are you sending a weekly update of confirmed shows to the PR agent and extended team?
- Are there any long-term activations you can be doing with a specific press outlet? Guest pieces, monthly mixes, etc.
- Establish any charitable causes close to the artist's heart and consider involvement.
- Create a list of brands your artist likes and could potentially work with.
- Keep up to date clothing measurements and shoe sizes for all artists.
- Send press from territories outside of PR agent's own and general news
- Guidelines for PR on how the artist works/ Only face to face, do they like skype or phone more than email interviews? What kind of interview are they into? etc....
- What are the expectations?

SALES OUTLETS

- Have you established a relationship with iTunes and/or Apple Music? Spotify? Amazon? Pandora? Soundcloud? TikTok? YouTube? Deezer?
- What's your artist's top sales outlet?
- How are you tracking sales per outlet?
- What are the top countries for your artist's monetized streams and track sales?

TRACKING

- Are you tracking single streams history?
- Album streams history?
- Single downloads history?
- Album downloads history?
- Have you checked SoundScan for sales data?
- Do you have access to the client's Spotify Fan Insights and Pandora AMP?

RADIO

- Who is working on your release to radio?
- Do you need an introduction to a radio promo team?
- What stations are supporting your release?
- Is there a radio plan created with targets and an end goal?
- Has your act created liners for key radio stations?
- Has your act created Pandora liners around their most recent release?
- Have you made your act available for interviews with key stations?
- Have you made your radio team and stations aware of upcoming shows in the market?
    - Have you offered tickets?
- Are you getting regular feedback from radio DJs on your release?

LIVE

- Are you tracking all sales markets?
- Are you aware of the top-selling acts in your market?
- Is there a portal where you can check ticket counts, or are you updated by your agent weekly?
- Are you aware of the key promoters in each of your touring markets?
- How is your act performing live compared to similar artists of a similar size?
- Are you requesting ticketing data (name, email, location, and whatever else they can provide) for every show?
- Are you building a mailing list in each market where you tour?
- Do you know what key festivals you want to play?
- Are you considering how doing a show in a market might affect your ability to perform at a key festival at a later date?
- Is the artist willing to invest any of their own money into individual show promotion?

SONGWRITING

PERFORMANCE RIGHTS

- Does your client belong to a performing rights organization (ASCAP, BMI, SESAC)?
- Is your client turning in set lists to their PRO post-show?
- Are all of your clients' most recent works updated with their PRO?
- If a client is unpublished, has publishing been registered with your PRO?
- Is your client claiming Neighboring Rights? Are they eligible?
- Is your client and their catalog registered with Sound Exchange?
- Do you know when you will receive statements from your PRO?
- Do you know who your rep is ,and are you actively engaged and seeking opportunities that may be available to your act?

PUBLISHING

- Does your client have a publishing deal?
- Do you know the MDRC?
- Do you know the publishing splits?
- Do you know the difference between the various publishing deals? Examples: Administrative Deal, Co-publishing deal, & full publishing deal?
- Do you know when you will receive statements from your publisher?
- Have writer splits been negotiated and contracted for all of your artist's works?
- Have split sheets been finalized before release of music?
- Has your publisher been updated on new releases and splits?
- Do you know what mechanical royalties are and how they work and are calculated?
- Are you familiar with the Harry Fox Agency?
- Do you know how a synchronization license works and how to procure one?
- Has your client recorded a cover? If so, has a license been granted for this work?
- Do you know what the Sync Department at your publishing company does? Are you in touch regularly?
- If your client is unpublished, is there an entity working to secure sync placements?
- Do you have a relationship with different sync companies?
- Do you know who your rep is, and are you actively engaged and seeking

- opportunities which may be available to your act?

TERMINOLOGY

- Do you know what a "work for hire" constitutes?
- Do you have a side artist agreement for any artists featuring on your release?
- Do you understand the term "points" and how they pertain to a master recording?
- Is the feature on your artist's work signed to a label?
- Do you have clearance from said label to release with "said" feature artist?
- Do you understand what makes up the key business aspects for a producer deal?
- Do you understand what makes up the key business points of a mixer deal?
1. Do you know the current mechanical statutory rate?

SAMPLES

- Does a body of work contain a sample?
- Have you checked that against a third party such as WhoSampled (http://www.whosampled.com/)?
- Have you gone through the sample clearance process yet?
- Are you aware of the companies that can help you clear a sample?
- Do you understand, when sampling, you need rights to use the original master recording?
- Have you considered having the sample re-sung or re-played to avoid paying to use the master?

COVERS

- Have you requested a Mechanical License from the Harry Fox Agency?
- Have you checked to make sure that your use is considered a cover and not a remix of the original work?

INTELLECTUAL PROPERTY

TRADEMARK

- Does your client have a trademark for their performing name?

- Does your client have a trademark/service mark for their text logo?
- Does your client have a trademark/service mark for their logo icon?
- Do you have copies of their trademark certificates?
- Does your client have a trademark attorney?
- Do you know what classes and categories you will be registering your trademark?
- Do you know what proof you need to provide to prove use in each of those classes?
- Do you know whether or not you can file for an extension on classes you don't currently use but may use in the future?
- Does your attorney have a system in place to remind you when those extensions are set to expire?
- Are you in contact with the attorney in case of conflicts, and are they updating you on any progress being made with registrations or other matters they may be handling for your client?

CREATIVE

PHOTO

- Are your artist's press shots up to date?
- Do you have a headshot with a blank background?
- Do you have a full-body shot with a blank background?
- Do you have 2+ personality shots (for editorial, exclusives, etc...)?
- Do you have 4-5 hi-res live shots that you have permission to use from the photographer and the promoter of the show?
- Do you have a shared folder of all raw images?
- Do you have a shared folder of approved live images for promoters and other outlets to use?
- Do you have permission to use images for all use? Or is the shoot based on promo-only use?
- Do you have the full exploitation rights doc signed by a photographer?
- How many shots has the photographer agreed to edit?
- Will you receive all raw shots as well as final edits?
- What are the terms if you decide to edit an existing raw shot?
- Is retouching included?
- Have you agreed on what images can be used in their portfolio?
- Do you have all the photo credit details? Are you providing PR/Press/Label etc....?

FOR PHOTOSHOOT

- What is your budget?
- Who is the photographer?
- What studio/space will you use?
- Does the location need to be rented?
- What are the hours of the shoot?
- Does the equipment need to be rented?
    - If so, who is covering the cost?
        - Is all equipment insured (incl. what the photographer owns)?
- Who is the stylist?
- Has the stylist requested a separate budget to pull clothing?
- Has the stylist asked for a budget for "restocking" items that were used in the shoot?
- Will the stylist be taking the artist shopping or bringing clothes?
- Who is the make-up artist?
    - Make sure the person is experienced in the hair types and skin colors of your client
- Do you need to provide catering?
- Has the entire photoshoot team discussed the creative?

VIDEO

- Do you have a video promo reel?
- Do you have all past video content backed up as hi-res files?
- Do you have a go-to videographer?
- Do you have a go-to video editor?
- Do you have a go-to video color corrector?
- Do you have a shared folder of all raw footage?
- Do you have a shared folder of approved live footage?

MUSIC VIDEO

- What is your budget?
- Are you going to use a music video commissioner?
    - If so, what's their rate?
    - Is it on top of or included within the budget?
- Will your artist be in the video?
- Have you sent out the concept/track for music video treatments?
- Has everyone on the team approved the treatment you've chosen?
- Who is the director?

- Who is the videographer?
- Who is the editor?
- Do you have the final video file specs needed for upload?
- Have you received a timeline from the director?
- Who is in charge of casting?
- Where will the video be shot?
- Do you have any necessary permits needed for the shooting location?
- Is there a production company involved?
- Does any equipment need to be rented?
- Is all equipment insured?
- Does a stylist need to be hired?
- Does a make-up artist need to be hired?
- Do you need to provide catering at the shoot?
- Will the editor provide 15-30 second clips to use for a promo before the video is released?
- Do you have a custom thumbnail image that can be used on Facebook and Youtube?
- Will there be a separate edit of the track for the music video?
- Does the editor have that version of the track before he starts the edit (WAV)?
- What is the agreement for edits, delivery date, etc...How many edits are allowed?

GRAPHIC DESIGN

- Do you have an artist logo?
    - Do you have the file formats you need?
- Do you have a font that goes with the artist logo well?
- Do you have the font file?
    - Do you have a license to use the font?
- Do you have a style guide?
- Do you have a go-to graphic designer?
- Do you have templates for any designs you re-use?
    - Do you have them easy to access and send out to those who need it?
- Are you aware of the current sizing for images on different web outlets AND social media?
- Does anyone on your team have a working knowledge of design software?
    - What are their limits?
- Does anyone on your team have a working knowledge of video editing?
    - What are their limitations?

ART FOR RELEASES

- Do you have freedom from the label to design your own?
- Does the label have any requirements for design content?
- Do you need designs for web use or physical packaging as well?
- What are the required specs for cover art and physical packaging art?
- Have you collected references to explain your vision to the designer?
- What is the deadline for release art submission?
- What is the designer's rate?
- Does their rate include multiple rounds of revisions?
- Does their rate include delivery of all editable design files and final art?
- Does their rate include delivery of all editable design files and final art?
- Do you have art for social media?
- Do you have art for advertising?
- Do you have the Pantone names for every color used in the design?

ART FOR LIVE SHOWS (WHEN NOT PROVIDED BY THE PROMOTER)

- Is the promoter covering the cost for design, or is your artist?
- Has the promoter sent you all assets they want to be included?
- If listing support, are you listening with artist logos or in a typeface?
- Do you have hi-res versions of support logos?
- Do you have approval from support on their billing and overall use of the logo?
- Will you create separate assets for each individual artist?
- Do you have all sizes needed to promote on social?
- Does your art for facebook meet the requirements for posting?
- Do you have custom video content that could be used for each individual show?
- Do you have non-text-heavy artwork for each show that can be used for engaging social posts?

MERCH

- Does your client have a merch vendor?
- Do you have a budget in mind for your initial merch order?
- Are you aware of the full range of services your merch vendor will facilitate?
- Are you aware of the fees associated with each service?
- Have you signed a written agreement with the merch company?
- Is your agreement exclusive or non-exclusive?
- Do you have NFTs/digital collectibles or Web3 asset ownership?

- Does your merch vendor handle domestic and foreign printing/online-store/live event services? If not, will you have a separate merch company for ROW sales?
- How has your client's merch been sold online so far?
- Do you have a geographic breakdown of where the artist's merchandise has been sold so far?
- Does your merch vendor handle vinyl production/sourcing?

MERCH DESIGN & PRODUCTION

- Does your merch company have a designer you will use, or are you hiring your own?
- Does the designer have experience designing for physical merchandise items?
- What printing method will you be using?
- Different methods have different limitations for design. What size/resolution does the printer need to execute the print properly?
- Does your client have merchandising rights for their artwork?
- Who is designing your merch?
- Does the designer have specs needed for printing from a printer or merch company?
- Do you have samples of the blanks?
- Will you be ordering samples of the printed item?
- What is the cost of each sample?
- Is the cost associated with the sample applied to your final order?
- Will you be digital printing (direct to garment) or screen printing?
- Are you fully informed of the costs for each printing method?
- Are you aware of the production timeline for each item?
  - Are you aware of rush fees?
- Are you checking in weekly with your merch company to make sure orders are on schedule?
- Do you have hi-res files for your designs?
- Have you approved all proofs before each item goes to print?
- Has your client signed off on all final designs and costs in your P.O.?
- What is the payment schedule?
- What is the billing schedule?
- Are you forecasting sales to determine printing quantities?
- How are you calculating the forecasted sales?
- Have you gotten your partner's opinion on the forecast?
- Are you doing pre-sales or waiting until you have physical inventory in hand?

ONLINE STORE

- Will your merch vendor build the online store?
- Is your merch vendor handling all online transactions?
- If not, what service will you use to manage the store?
- What is the merchant processing fee for your vendor?
- Does your merch vendor handle shipping and fulfillment?
- What is the merchant customer service policy?
- Do they have a reputation of being particularly good or bad from a customer service perspective?
- Once the order is placed, how long will your merch company take to ship?
- Are you aware of the timeline for designing, printing, and shipping each merch item?
- Does your merch vendor charge a fee if you choose to use an outside supplier but sell on your merch store?
- Can your merch vendor create coupon codes to market sales around holidays and special events?
- Backend to view sales and statistics?
- Do you have assets to post on social to promote new products?
- Do you have the flexibility to sell your merch on platforms like Facebook?
- Have you set up a merch offer on Spotify through your artist's Bandpage?

TOURING MERCH

- Will you be providing your own merch seller, or does the venue provide one?
- Does your merch vendor require that one of their team members sells on tour?
- Will your merch vendor provide a seller for you, or do you need to hire one on your own?
- If paying for your own vendor, how are you paying them day rate, week rate, hourly, etc.........?
- What is the merch split with the venue, and have you tried to negotiate the rate down?
- Does your merch vendor have the contact info for each venue to advance merch?
- What is the shipping cost to send merch to each show?
- Will your merch vendor organize and advance all of your live/touring sales?
- Will your merch vendor be organizing and advancing all shipping for live shows?

- Will your merch vendor organize and advance all of your live sale transactions and accounting?
- Is there a system in place where you are alerted when stock levels are low during a tour?
- Are things like a table, lighting, and clips included in your rider?
- Will the venue provide a cash drawer and credit card machine?
- Are you responsible for supplying the cash drawer and credit card option (Square etc...)
- If you leave the country with merch or gear, do you have a carnet filled out listing all items?
- Are you aware that you pay tax in some countries when you enter the country with merch, regardless of what is actually sold?
- Are you getting a nightly report post-show on sales?
- Is that lining up with your forecast?
- How and what are you paying your merch seller?
- Are you running a forecast of sales? Positive or negative forecast?
- What is the forecast for cost per head? Who is calculating and how?
- Have you gotten other people's opinions on the forecast?
- Can you share merch costs such as shipping/merch seller/transactions with another act on the bill?

DAILY/WEEKLY/MONTHLY CHECKLISTS

DAILY

- Check touring schedule - have shows been advanced, added to socials, flier approved, on sale, etc
- Check social pages - any trending topics related to your artist? How is the engagement on the page?
- Are you reaching your social media goals?
- Take ten to fifteen minutes a day to comb through industry news
- Speak with agent(s) about upcoming shows and outstanding offers that need confirmation, and get ticket counts for upcoming shows.
- Review your artist's twelve-month plan. What action items can be accomplished today?
- Ten-minute huddle with your team to ensure key goals are being met. Speak with your artist to make sure they are on track with current goals and plans.
- Create a top 5 to-do list for the day, items that must be checked off by end of day.
- Check tracking for any important items being shipped.
- If your artist is on tour: Confirm all travel plans are on schedule, confirm shows have been performing well with artist and agent, and update the team on performance.
- Check the social networks of your artist. What is the general fan sentiment, has there been any spike in numbers, have any influencers connected with them, etc.

WEEKLY

- Track ticket sales to ensure shows are performing well and are on track. If show sales are low, figure out a plan to enhance sales, contests, extra marketing, etc.
- Schedule social media posts for the week and adjust accordingly.
- Check week-over-week social growth for the artists (Resources include Chartmetric, Next Big Sound, or each individual social network's own analytics).
- Speak to the label to get an update on the project.
- Speak to the agent about new offers.
- Speak with the PR rep about progress.
- Confirm that artists are aware of their schedule for the week.
- Nudge artist on anything ongoing that you need from them (interviews to

complete, radio liners, etc.)

- Send the entire team (label, PR, merch company, etc...) a list of confirmed show dates and project updates (streams, sales, radio updates, etc.)
- Hold team management meetings to review each project in depth.
- Make sure merch company is advancing all confirmed shows and shipments are on schedule.
- Check online merch sales and discuss if there is extra marketing needed to move the product.
- Check with the merch company that any ongoing production is on schedule.
- Check streams and music sales for the week. Has there been any noticeable rise or drop in a particular DSP?
  - Can you identify why?
  - Make sure all upcoming shows have signed off on your technical rider.
  - Scan through any shared folders for new items, items that may have accidentally been removed, etc.
- Go through your company's Digital Media update and make sure you are utilizing new tools and updating your artist's outlets accordingly.
- Make sure the booking team is updating the master show tracker with the offer status.
- Assess what other relevant/comparable artists are doing marketing-wise and performing online.
- Find time to discuss any big-picture developments with your senior management.
- Review social content for the week to see what has performed well and the types of content fans are organically engaging with.

MONTHLY

- Update revenue tracker with live income.
- Make sure the revenue tracker has been updated with record sales income.
- Update revenue tracker with digital monetization income.
- Make sure the revenue tracker has been updated with publishing income.
- Create social media outline for next month.
- Keep a list of goals and targets to reach each month.
- Get a report from the merch company on show sales and discuss if items/quantities need to be adjusted going forward.
- Update one sheet & artist bio with adjusted social numbers and updated blurbs, contacts.
- Make sure PR, booking, and the entire team have updated press assets. Hold a meeting with the whole team to review the past month and the

- month ahead.
- Make sure all masters are registered with PRO, and there were no issues with your previous submissions.
- Follow up on all outstanding invoices.
- Review the month ahead and note what agreements or contracts are up for renewal and require attention.

PLANNING

GENERAL

- Do you have a 3, 6, and 12-month plan ready for your artist?
- Have you identified the short-term and long-term goals that your client wants to achieve?
- Have financial goals been established with your artist and team?
- Have you created a timeline to ensure you reach your 3, 6, and 12-month goals.
- Have you reached out to your partners for feedback on your plan and additional ideas?

VOL. 2 KEY UPDATES & ADDITIONS

MARKETING > MUSIC RELEASE ASSETS

- Have you created short-form vertical video content (15–60 sec) for each song?
- Is there a 9:16 optimized video version for Reels/TikTok/YT Shorts?
- Have you considered AI-generated visual assets (e.g. Luma, Runway, Sora) for storytelling?

BUSINESS MANAGEMENT

- Have you explored automating payouts and splits using tools like Stem, Infinite Catalog, or Trolley?
- Have you integrated AI tools to assist with revenue tracking or expense categorization?
- Has a fractional CFO or advisor been hired or consulted?

TOURING > TRAVEL

- Are you tracking carbon emissions or offsetting large tour footprints?
- Have you registered your artist for Clear or international equivalents (like Nexus)?

PAID ONLINE MARKETING

- Are you running performance creative tests using AI tools (e.g. pencil.ai, adcreative.ai)?
- Are you using Spark Ads or TikTok Creator Marketplace for UGC seeding?

SOCIAL NETWORK/STREAMING

- Have you created a Discord server or SMS community for core fans?
- Is your artist publishing content on Threads or Kick?
- Have you developed custom AR filters or IG effects tied to your release or tour?

PLANNING > GENERAL

- Is there a quarterly review process built in with key partners?
- Do you have a standing team sync (weekly or biweekly) for performance review?
- Have you scheduled an annual offsite/creative retreat to plan long-term brand goals?